Decorating Christmas Cakes

Spectacular Festive Designs

Dedication

To the late Jean Bradford, Paul's Gran, who started Paul decorating cakes at a young age and was a continual pillar of support, and to David's parents, June and Eric, who would have been proud beyond belief to have seen this book.

Decorating Christmas Cakes

Spectacular Festive Designs

PAUL BRADFORD AND DAVID BRICE

Search Press

First published in Great Britain 2013

Search Press Limited
Wellwood, North Farm Road,
Tunbridge Wells, Kent TN2 3DR

Illustrations and text copyright ©
Paul Bradford and David Brice 2013

Photographs by Roddy Paine
Photographic Studios
apart from the materials photographs on
pages 8–11 by Paul Doffman

Photographs and design copyright ©
Search Press Ltd, 2013

ISBN: 978-1-84448-883-4

The Publishers and author can accept no
responsibility for any consequences arising
from the information, advice or instructions
given in this publication.

Suppliers
If you have difficulty in obtaining any of the
materials and equipment mentioned in this
book, then please visit the Search Press
website for details of suppliers:
www.searchpress.com

You are invited to visit the authors' website:
www.designer-cakes.com

Printed in China

Acknowledgements

Special thanks to Sophie Kersey and Roddy Paine.
We would also like to thank David Oliphant who took
the chance and gave us the opportunity, and
Cecilia Young who gave Paul the knowledge and
inspiration. Thanks also to Mrs Jones for her patience
in tweaking the cake recipe.

Contents

Introduction

Paul started making cakes every Saturday afternoon with his Gran at a very young age. He enjoyed it so much that when his teacher asked everyone in class, at age twelve, what they wanted to do when they grew up, he proudly announced that he wanted to have his own cake shop making speciality cakes. This ambition certainly stood out from the crowd and received much jeering from his classmates.

Paul couldn't wait to leave school and took a bakery course at Telford College in Edinburgh, which resulted in a placement at Oliphant's bakery in Linlithgow. On completing the course, he was offered a permanent job at Oliphant's where he worked in the confectionery department before taking a job in Glasgow at Top Tier Designer Cakes. His plan was to learn as much as he could so that in five or so years' time he would have sufficient experience to start up on his own.

Just under a year into this job, David Oliphant offered Paul the opportunity to open a small unit behind a bakery he had just taken on. With very little experience, but loads of ambition and enthusiasm, Paul said 'yes' and opened in May 2002. David and Paul had shared a flat in Glasgow and at that time David worked with the Ministry of Defence. By 2005 David was working as a speech writer in the Scottish Government when, to everyone's amazement, he took a career break to oversee the growth of the business.

The business grew rapidly to have seven outlets employing thirty-five staff. During this time Paul made cakes for the Queen, Prince Charles, Prince Albert of Monaco and a host of celebrities. However, both Paul and David knew that teaching was the direction they wanted to move towards, so they sold their designer cakes and cupcake café businesses in 2011 and 2012.

With his experience in creating 'wow' factor cakes that needed to be commercially viable, Paul quickly found his niche with some amazing designs which he started teaching at his Sugarcraft School, where he and David also film and produce online courses. He was quickly recognised for his talents and was invited to teach in Rome, Milan, Madrid, Barcelona, Monte Carlo, Zurich, Cologne and throughout the UK.

The Christmas cakes in this book have all been designed with fun in mind, since being of a positive, happy mindset is hugely important to the end result when you are making cakes. The basic skills needed are all explained step by step at the beginning to get you started. The cakes display a variety of styles and techniques, from cute and funny modelled characters to stunning, intricate designs, so there should be something for everyone. You can have a bit of fun altering the designs to your specific requirements and pop the odd penguin or snowman here or there to add your own personal touch.

Above: detail from the Santa Surprise! cake on page 84 and opposite: the Christmas Wedding cake on page 68.

Materials

Cake construction

Cake

This is the single most important ingredient, as there is no point in decorating a spectacular cake if the cake itself is dry or tasteless. We use an oil-based recipe which works well, giving a very moist cake, which is easy to carve and has a shelf life of seven to ten days. The recipe is on page 12.

Ganache

Chocolate ganache gives a far smoother effect and is more temperature tolerant than buttercream for layering and covering cakes in preparation for the sugarpaste. With the higher cocoa content of dark chocolate, it allows for a faster setting temperature and higher melting temperature. This is especially useful in warmer climates or during the summer months as it significantly reduces the chance of bulges appearing, usually caused by melting buttercream. Ganache acts more as a glue to keep the cake together. Unless otherwise stated, the ganache used in the projects is made with dark chocolate. The recipe is on page 13.

Royal icing

This is a very versatile cake decorating medium. It is used here as the glue to hold decorations together or for piping on patterns or details.

Cake boards and cards

Used for sitting the cakes on and as separators between tiers.

Icing sugar

Used both in the making of buttercream and to spread on surfaces before rolling out sugarpaste, flower paste or modelling chocolate.

Cone

This is used to shape the top of the cone-shaped cakes before they are covered. You can use either a pre-made polystyrene cone or make one out of card.

Cake covering

Sugarpaste

This is available in white and a range of colours, and is sometimes referred to as fondant. It is used for covering cakes and for modelling. It is usually sold in 250g (8½oz) packs, so the 'you will need' lists in the projects state this amount, though you may sometimes need less.

CMC

This is an edible synthetic powdered gum which is mixed through sugarpaste (1 teaspoon of CMC to 350g/12oz sugarpaste) to make the sugarpaste more pliable and set it more firmly. You can also use Tylose, sometimes known as gum tragacanth.

Modelling chocolate

Sometimes referred to as chocolate plastique, this is available commercially in dark, milk or white chocolate. It is excellent for modelling as it is stronger and more flexible than sugarpaste and can be formed into a variety of shapes and structures that cannot be easily accomplished with other softer edible materials.

Flower paste

An extremely useful medium for modelling, making flowers and casting moulds. It is widely available and often referred to as gum paste.

Sugarpaste, flower paste and modelling chocolate.

Tools

Modelling tools

These include a ball/bone tool for making sockets and rounded holes; a cone tool for making small point indentations and sockets; a Dresden tool for lining, shaping, sculpting and making eye sockets; a quilting tool which is ideal for straight lines and to give a stitch effect; a scriber tool for removing air bubbles; and a smile tool for giving a smile effect on models and decorative patterns.

Brushes

A selection of small paintbrushes are useful for getting the finer detail.

Metal ruler and scraper

Used for smoothing the ganache on to the cake.

Wires

Thin 20 and 26 gauge wires are used in a number of projects to shape and hold the sugarpaste in place.

Pasta maker

Used to achieve a thinner and consistent finish when rolling out the modelling chocolate.

Cutting tools

Various cutters

Holly, snowflake, star, petal, blossom and fluted oval cutters, a straight-edged scallop and a gingerbread man cutter are used in these projects to cut out sugarpaste shapes.

Knives

A large knife is needed for carving cakes. You will also need a small sharp knife for cutting sugarpaste and large and small palette knives for applying and smoothing ganache. A serrated knife is also essential for the cake decorator's toolbox.

Wire cutters

These are useful for cutting through dowels and wires.

Scissors

These are used for snipping into sugarpaste, for instance when shaping fir trees. They are also used for cutting out templates.

Edible colourings

A range of food-safe colouring materials are used in these projects and are widely available. We have used edible powder food colours in a range of colours, edible lustre sprays, edible and non-toxic glitter, edible lustre powders, clear edible glaze spray, silver, gold, red and autumn leaf edible paste colour, silver and gold liquid paint and edible white crystal flakes. Food grade alcohol or vodka is used to apply some colours. Coloured metallic, silver and gold balls are used to add colour, detail and shine.

Finishing touches

Impression mats

These are used to add texture to sugarpaste to give a very quick and effective decorative finish.

Diamante strip

This provides a non-edible element of 'bling' to a cake board.

Edible pen

For marking models and making small, detailed decorations.

Ribbons

For decorating the rim of the cake board. Attach them with non-toxic glue stick.

Circle cutters

These are used for cutting sugarpaste in a wide range of sizes.

Crimped silver wire

This is used as a final decoration for some cakes.

Other materials

Turntable

This gives the height and motion to help with many cake decorating tasks.

Dowels

Wooden or plastic dowels can both be cut to size using wire cutters. They are needed to support the tiered cakes and other decorations.

Piping bag and nozzles

Many decorating tasks require a piping bag and the different nozzles will achieve a variety of finishes.

Pastry brush

This will help give a smooth finish to the ganache.

Smoothers

Essential for achieving the smooth finish on the cakes. Working them both together helps to achieve sharp corners when needed.

Rolling pins

For rolling out the sugarpaste to the desired depth. The ends also come in useful when creating round shapes and indents.

Garlic press

A great tool to achieve long thin sugarpaste strands, which are ideal as hair on the models.

Food bags

For storing sugarpaste and preparing the rose decorations.

Spaghetti

To support decorations and keep them in place.

Edible wafer paper

Sometimes known as rice paper, this decoration is used to decorate an entire cake in the Angel Cake project on page 32.

Tweezers

Used for placing small decorative items on the cakes and for creating the effect of fur.

Bamboo skewers

For supporting models and other decorations.

Florist tape

Used to cover the wires, ensuring that there is no direct contact with the cake.

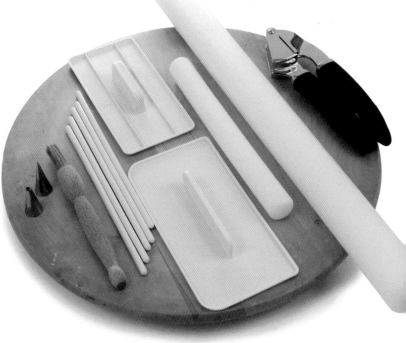

Recipes

Cake

A full video on the making of this cake is available on our website. The recipe below is enough to produce a 25.4cm (10in) plus a 15.3cm (6in) round cake, or the same batch will produce one 25.4cm (10in) square cake.

330g (12oz) unsalted butter
330g (12oz) dark chocolate (60% cocoa if possible)
9 tsp (45ml/1½fl oz) instant coffee
240ml (8fl oz) water
75g (2½oz) cocoa powder
187g (6½oz) plain flour
187g (6½oz) self-raising flour
1 tsp bicarbonate of soda
720g (1lb 9oz) golden caster sugar
6 large eggs
10½ tsp (55.5ml/2 fl oz) vegetable oil (rapeseed preferred but not essential)
165ml (5½fl oz) buttermilk

• **Chocolate sauce** Place the butter, chocolate, coffee and water into a pan on a medium heat. Slowly stir until everything blends together then put to one side.
• **Egg batter** Start with the eggs in a bowl. Add the buttermilk, then the vegetable oil and whisk together for 3 minutes, then put to one side.
• **Dry ingredients** Mix together the cocoa powder, caster sugar, plain and self-raising flour and bicarbonate of soda.
• Pour the chocolate sauce into the egg batter and whisk it through.
• Adding a little at a time, pour the chocolate batter into the dry ingredients, mixing through each time. Once combined, whisk quickly for 2 minutes.
• Line cake tins (sides and base) with greaseproof paper then fill them to about half way. Place in a pre-heated oven at 150°C/300°F/Gas Mark 2 for 2 hours. If baking two cakes, put the bigger cake on the higher shelf.
• You can pour Irish cream liqueur over a finished, cooled cake to add moistness and flavour.

Tip

For best results if you need to carve the cake, freeze and defrost it first.

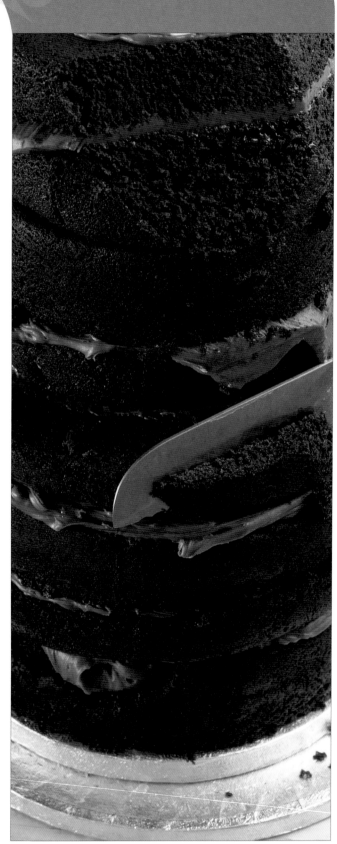

Chocolate ganache

Once you start layering cakes with chocolate ganache you won't look back as it gives a far sharper finish than buttercream, allowing neat edges. You can use dark, milk or white chocolate but it is best to go with dark as the higher cocoa content gives a quicker setting time and lower melting temperature, which is perfect when working in warmer climates. Dark and milk chocolate ganache is made from boiling cream then mixing in the chocolate with a ratio of 1.13 litres (2 pints) cream to 454g (1lb) chocolate. These amounts will make 1.56kg (3½lb) of ganache. For white ganache, increase the chocolate by a third to 595g (1lb 5oz).

Royal icing

Using these quantities produces nearly 1kg (2lb 3oz) of royal icing.

20g (¾oz) egg albumen
133ml (4½ fl oz) water
800g (1lb 12oz) icing sugar

- Mix together the albumen and water using your mixer.
- Add half the icing sugar and mix until fully mixed through.
- Add the remaining icing sugar a bit at a time then beat (on the slowest speed) until the icing is at the desired consistency.
- To prevent the royal icing drying out, cover with a clean, damp cloth or tea towel and overwrap in plastic food wrap.
- If the icing softens, add a little extra icing sugar and re-beat.

Buttercream

500g (1lb 1½oz) unsalted butter
1kg (2lb 3oz) icing sugar

- Ensure the butter is at room temperature. Put the butter in the mixing bowl then slowly add the icing sugar on a low speed.
- Once it is all mixed through, mix on medium speed for three minutes.

Techniques

Modelling shapes with sugarpaste

It is worth spending time to get the basic shapes and techniques right before embarking on the projects in this book. These steps show you how to tackle figures, a small animal and making a rose.

Rolling a ball

Roll the sugarpaste between your hands to make a ball.

Making a cone

Roll a ball of sugarpaste, then angle your hand as shown to roll it into a cone. The pointed shape begins to emerge.

Making a teardrop

Begin in the same way as for a cone, but round the narrow end rather than rolling it to a point.

Making a sausage shape

1 Start rolling with your fingers together.

2 As you continue rolling, open your fingers out. This keeps the width of the sausage even.

3 Continue rolling with your fingers wide apart.

4 To finish the sausage, use a smoother to perfect it.

The four basic shapes: clockwise from top left: a cone, ball, sausage and teardrop.

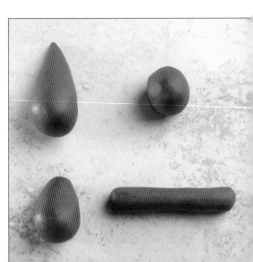

Making a Santa

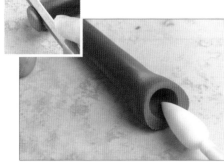

1 Make a red sugarpaste sausage and press on the middle as you roll so that the ends flare out.

2 Trim both ends with a knife and hollow them out with a cone tool.

3 Fold the shape in two to create the legs and pinch the fold.

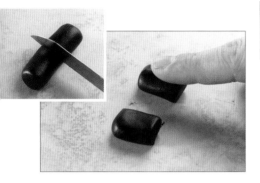

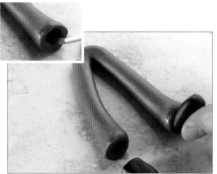

4 Roll a black sugarpaste sausage and cut it in half. Soften the ends and press in the middle to make boots.

5 Brush water in the sockets and push in the black boots.

6 Use the back of the knife to imprint heels.

7 Make white sausages for fur, brush with water and attach. Trim the ends.

8 Brush the ends with water and press to stick. Texture with the small end of a ball tool to look like fur.

9 Make a red cone body and try it for size on the legs. Cut off the base.

10 Smooth the shape with your fingers and pinch out the bottom to hollow it out slightly.

11 Brush the body with water and stick on the legs. Push a stick of spaghetti down to the worktop and snap off the top, leaving a length sticking out.

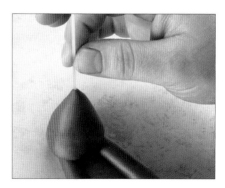

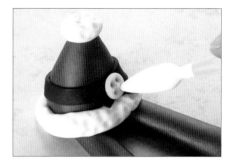

12 Attach and texture fur round the body as for the legs. Feed a ball of white sugarpaste over the spaghetti and texture to make fur.

13 Roll a black sausage flat and cut it into a belt shape. Brush water on to the body, stick it on and trim it.

14 Roll a tiny yellow ball, flatten to make a buckle, wet and press it on. Use a cone tool to make holes.

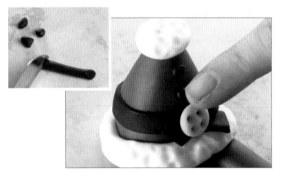

15 Roll a tiny black sausage and cut buttons from it. Wet the body and push the buttons on.

16 Brush water on the body where the arms will go to make it tacky. Roll a long red sausage, trim the ends and cut it in half. Try it for size and cut it to match.

17 Taper each arm at one end and push the cone tool in the wide ends to make sockets. Make two little green cones for gloves. Brush water in the sockets.

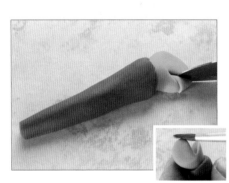

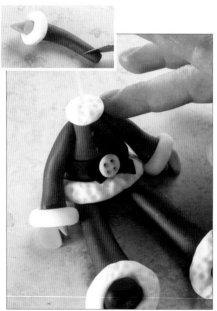

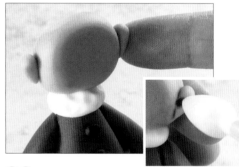

18 Push in the gloves. Press them down on the work surface and cut a 'v' shape with a knife to make thumbs. Round off the shape with a damp brush.

19 Make, attach and texture a fur trim as for the legs and body. Cut the arm at an angle to fit the body and press on to the tacky surface to stick it.

20 Mix half teddy bear brown to half flesh tone sugarpaste, roll into a ball for the head. Check for size, then flatten it. Push the head on to the spaghetti stick. Make two little cones as for the gloves and stick them on for ears with the wide end at the top. Place a finger behind each ear and make a hole with the cone tool. Roll a small ball of the same colour, dampen the face and push on for the nose.

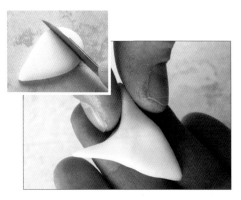

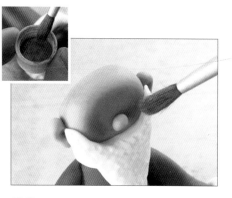

21 Make a white cone for the beard, flatten it and cut off the round end. Pinch the edges to shape to create sideburns.

22 Press the beard on to the face and texture it as for the fur, but with the quilting tool.

23 Shake a bottle of rose edible powder food colour and tap it upside down. Take colour from the lid with a dry no. 6 paintbrush, brush the excess off on your hand then dust Santa's cheeks.

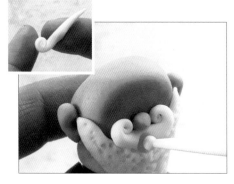

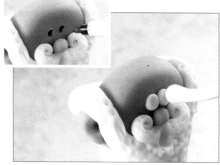

24 Brush water above the beard. Roll a pea-sized ball of white sugarpaste into a sausage, taper and curl the ends. Press on. Push a ball tool in to make the mouth saying 'ho ho ho!'

25 For a hatless Santa, make a long tapered white sausage, wrap around the head and texture with the quilting tool for hair.

26 Eyes can be done with one of two methods. First, dot them on with a black edible pen. Alternatively, roll tiny balls of white and push them on to a dampened surface with a ball tool, then mark pupils with a food pen.

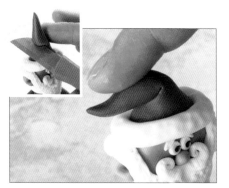

27 Make little white sausages for eyebrows, stick on then texture with a quilting tool.

28 To make a hat, make a red cone, cut off the bottom and shape as in step 10. Add a white trim as before and place on the head. Slice into the hat so that you can bend it.

The finished Santa.

Making a penguin

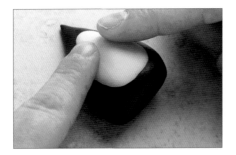

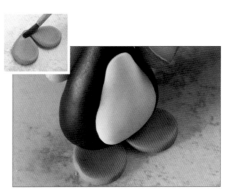

1 Make a cone in black for the body and flatten it. Make a small white cone, flatten it and press it on to the body. Smooth it in with two fingers.

2 Roll out orange sugarpaste 2mm (¹/₁₆in) thick and cut out two feet with a petal cutter.

3 Push the feet together and brush them with water. Press on the body. Push dry spaghetti through to the work surface as for Santa.

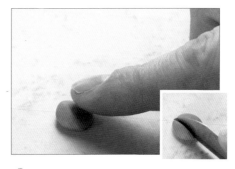

4 Make a black sausage for arms, roll flat and cut in half. Brush the body with water so that it goes tacky. Trim the arms and cut the shoulders at an angle.

5 Place the arms on the tacky surface on the body and curl them up.

6 Make a black ball to size and push it on the spaghetti for the head. Make a small orange ball and flatten one side for the beak. Cut off the back.

7 Press on the beak.

8 Make little white eyeballs as for Santa. Push them on and press them with a bone tool. Add pupils with black edible pen.

The finished penguin.

Making a rose

1 Make a cone for the base. This is in jade.

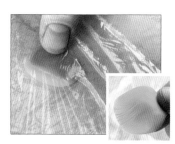

2 Make a sausage and cut it into eleven equal-sized pieces. Lay them out as shown, ready to make layers of petals.

3 Roll a piece into a ball then a flat sausage, and place it in a food bag. Press down half to make the petal shape and to impress the creases from the bag. Lift the petal out by the fat end.

4 Place the petal on the base halfway up the petal's width, and curl it round. Pinch the first half in place.

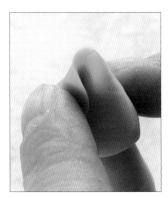

5 Curl the second half round over the first.

6 Pinch a 'waist' in the rose.

7 Turn the base so that the join is facing away. Make another, wider petal and press it on 2mm (¹/₁₆in) higher than the first. Wrap the left side round and press in place.

8 Make a standard petal and tuck it inside the open flap of the wide petal. Pinch it closed and wrap the new petal round.

9 Fold the petal back gently to create the shape. This completes layers one and two as laid out in step 2.

10 Repeat the same process for layers three and four, placing each layer a little higher and tucking subsequent petals inside. Shape the petals by folding them back a little.

11 Cut the rose off the base with a knife.

The finished rose.

Layering and covering a cake with ganache

Layering the cake with ganache and then covering it before the sugarpaste goes on can seem time-consuming, but the effort is certainly worth it as you will achieve a sharp finish time and time again. Ganache also keeps well and tastes wonderful.

1 Level the top of the cake with a large serrated knife. Start from halfway across and cut into the 'hill'.

2 Trim down the sides to level them, then cut the cake in half. Mark the side with the back of the knife so that you will know how to reassemble the cake.

3 Spread a blob of ganache on a cake board and place the bottom half of the cake on top. Pour Irish cream liqueur on top and spread it in with a palette knife.

4 Place a generous blob of ganache on the cake and spread with a palette knife. Put on the top, matching up the marks made in step 2. Press down to level the cake.

5 Smooth the ganache coming out of the sides and put the cake in the fridge to set. On a turntable, spread ganache round the sides of the cake.

6 Spread the ganache so that it stands higher than the cake.

7 Dip a metal scraper in boiling water. Begin with your scraper hand at 12 o'clock and your other hand on the turntable at 1 o'clock. Turn and scrape to smooth the ganache.

8 Hold the metal scraper vertical to check that the scraped sides of the cake are completely straight. If not, go round again applying more pressure at the top or bottom. Chill in the fridge.

9 Take the cake out of the fridge after ten minutes. Dip a palette knife in hot water. Push it away from you to cut off the lip of the ganache sides. This creates a sharp finish.

10 Place a generous dollop of ganache on top of the cake and smooth it with a palette knife.

11 Take the cake off the turntable. Wet a metal ruler in hot water. Stand with one foot behind the other and use the ruler to smooth the top of the ganache.

12 Back on the turntable, take off the excess ganache with the metal scraper as before. Place the cake back in the fridge until it sets again.

13 Use the palette knife dipped in hot water to cut off the excess ganache from the top.

14 Shave away any lumps or bumps with the wet palette knife.

15 Dip a pastry brush in hot water and give the ganache a final smooth. This also makes it sticky ready for the sugarpaste covering.

The cake covered with ganache.

Icing the cake

1 Sprinkle icing sugar over the work surface, then roll out the sugarpaste, reshaping it as you turn it to roll, to keep it round. When it reaches a certain size, pick it up on the rolling pin to turn it. Roll it to 4mm (¹/₈in) thick.

2 Lift the sugarpaste on the rolling pin and cover the cake.

3 Open out the pleats.

4 Using just two fingers, gently attach the sugarpaste at the top. Take your time and continue gently massaging the sugarpaste on to the cake.

5 Use the rim of the smoother to indent the base of the cake where it meets the board.

6 Cut between the cake and the board with the point of a knife, and remove the excess sugarpaste.

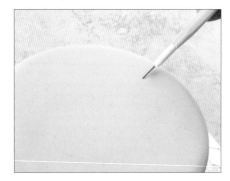

7 If there are any air bubbles in the sugarpaste, push in a scriber tool at an angle.

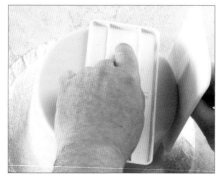

8 Smooth the sides and top with smoothers.

The iced cake.

Icing and trimming the board

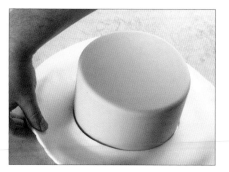

1 Sprinkle icing sugar, then roll out white sugarpaste, reshaping after each turn to keep the round shape until it reaches the desired size, 5cm (2in) larger in diameter than the cake board and 4mm (¹/₈in) thick. Wet the board with water. For a cake 15.3cm (6in) in diameter, cut out a circle in the middle of 10cm (4in) diameter. I do this freehand. Take out the central circle of sugarpaste.

2 Lift the ring of sugarpaste on the rolling pin and offer it up to the cake, then place it over the top.

3 Gently stretch the ring over the top of the cake and the edge of the board.

4 Gently soften the sugarpaste on to the board with your hands, and push it in towards the cake to create a perfect edge.

5 Smooth with the smoother to get rid of any fingerprints.

6 Go round with a clean, sharp knife to trim off the excess sugarpaste.

7 Peel off the excess sugarpaste, then soften the edges of the iced board with your fingers to round it.

8 Apply non-toxic glue stick to the edge of the cake board and pull ribbon round it. Cut the ends at an angle and stick down for a neat finish.

The iced cake and board.

Snowball Fight

You don't need to be a child to enjoy a snowball fight. This cake is full of winter fun and is made using simple cake covering and modelling techniques; the impact is in the detail. You can create your own take on the scene by changing the positioning, look and clothes of the models.

You will need

15.3cm (6in) round cake

25.4cm (10in) round cake board

600g (1lb 5oz) ganache

Large serrated knife

Silver ribbon and non-toxic glue stick

Sugarpaste: 1kg (2lb 3oz) pale blue, 250g (8½oz) each of white, black, orange, red, bottle green, purple, fuchsia pink, teddy bear brown, flesh tone, yellow, Atlantic blue, chocolate brown and Lincoln green

Rolling pins

Paintbrushes: sizes 2 and 00

Turntable

Sharp knife

100g (3½oz) royal icing

Small piping bag with a 1.5 plain nozzle

60g (2oz) white sugarpaste with CMC

Bamboo skewer

Wire cutters

Spaghetti

26 gauge wire and brown florist tape

Smallest circle cutter

Scriber

Dresden tool

Quilting tool

Bone tool

Dark brown edible paste colour and vodka or food grade alcohol

Pearl white edible lustre powder

Smile tool

Red paste colour

Rose edible powder food colour

Garlic press

Edible glitter

Food bag

Edible white crystal flakes

1 Follow pages 20–23 to ganache a 15.3cm (6in) cake and ice it with pale blue sugarpaste. Ice the board with white sugarpaste and trim it with a silver ribbon. Allow to dry for at least half a day before decorating. Brush water on the top of the iced cake with a paintbrush.

2 Roll out white sugarpaste to 3mm (⅛in) thick and cut a rough circle 20.3cm (8in) in diameter.

3 Lift the circle over the cake so that it hangs down equally over the sides and smooth it carefully with your hands.

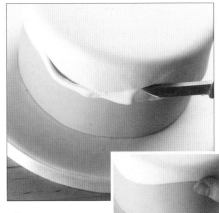

4 Place the cake on a.turntable. As you turn it, cut a wavy line in the edge of the white sugarpaste, making sure you match up the ends. Soften the edges with your thumb.

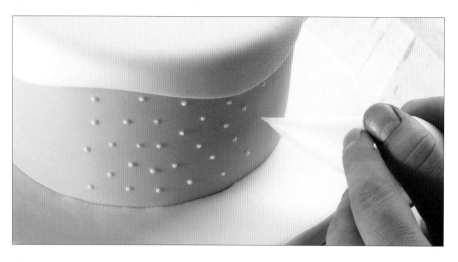

5 Use a small piping bag and royal icing to pipe dots of white on to the blue sides of the cake. You can use them to hide any flaws.

The snowman

6 Knead CMC into white sugarpaste or use white modelling paste. Roll a thick sausage and cut it into three pieces in descending size. Roll them into the balls for the snowman and leave them to dry for two hours.

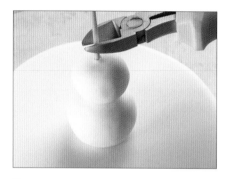

7 Wet the middle of the cake. Place the biggest ball on top. Push in a bamboo skewer, right down through the ball and cake to the cake board. Wet the first ball and place the second on top, pushing it over the skewer. Trim the bamboo skewer with wire cutters, leaving a bit sticking out for the head.

8 Make black buttons in the same way as Santa's (page 16, step 15), plus two more for eyes, and a row of smaller ones for a mouth.

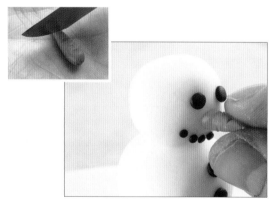

9 Roll a tiny orange sugarpaste cone for the carrot nose. Use a knife to add texture, then cut off the thick end, wet the face and stick on the nose.

10 Make the scarf as for Santa's belt (page 16, step 13) but in red sugarpaste, and attach, first brushing water round the neck. Trim to fit.

11 Cut two tails as for the scarf and indent the ends with a knife to make a fringe. Attach one over the join of the scarf, and curl up the end with a brush.

12 Lift the scarf a little and prop it up to dry by pushing in a stick of spaghetti.

13 Roll out black sugarpaste to 2mm (¹/₁₆in) and cut a circle with the smallest circle cutter. Brush water on the snowman's head, stick it on and leave to dry.

14 Roll out a black sugarpaste sausage, taper it at one end and trim to size. Pinch out the wider end to hollow it a bit with your fingers. Stick spaghetti in the head and push on the top of the hat.

15 Make two tiny cones of bottle green sugarpaste, indent down the centres and along the sides to make holly. Wet the hat, stick on the holly and add tiny red sugarpaste berries. Use a scriber to indent tiny holes for the berry points.

16 Wrap half width brown florist tape round 26 gauge wire to make the snowman's stick arm, then attach another piece and twist it to add a finger.

17 Repeat to make further fingers for the stick, then push it into the snowman's body.

The girl figure

18 Begin the girl figure by making her shoes. Make a sausage of black sugarpaste, cut a circle and flatten it, then indent a line around it for the sole.

19 Make smaller black balls and push these on top of the shoe bases.

20 Wet the snow surface of the iced cake board next to the cake and stick on the shoes.

  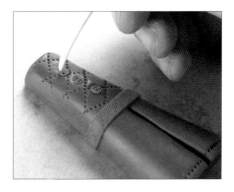

21 To make the body and trousers, make a purple sausage, tapered at one end. Trim at the side end and pinch out to shape. Indent with the Dresden tool to separate the legs. Check the height against the cake as the finished figure will lean on the top.

22 Use the quilting tool round the bottoms of the legs for stitching, then make a criss-cross pattern round the top in the same way.

23 Make a belt in fuchsia pink sugarpaste in the same way as Santa's (page 16, step 13). Add buttons as for Santa's buttons (page 16, step 15) but dot the buttonholes with the other end of the quilting tool.

24 Place the body over the shoes and push a stick of spaghetti down to the board to anchor it. Place spaghetti behind the body to support it while it dries.

25 Make tails for the belt as for the snowman's scarf (steps 11 to 12) and attach them, but without spaghetti support. Make a fuchsia pink ball for the collar, flatten it and push it on the spaghetti coming out of the neck.

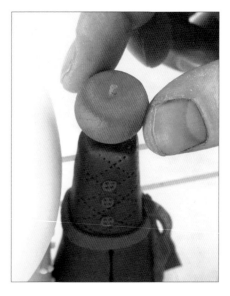

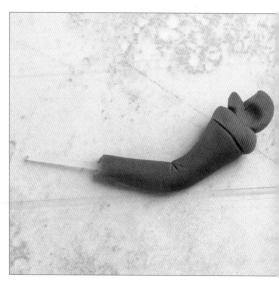

26 Push on a ball of purple sugarpaste for the neck.

27 Make arms and hands as for Santa (page 16, steps 16–18), with purple arms and fuchsia pink fur trims and hands. Bend the first arm and mark little creases with a knife at the elbow. Make holes for sockets with a bone tool. Wet the white sugarpaste and place the arm leaning on the cake as shown.

28 Stick spaghetti in the other arm and leave it to dry, ready to attach when the rest of the figure is finished.

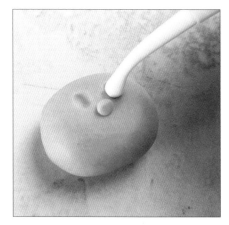

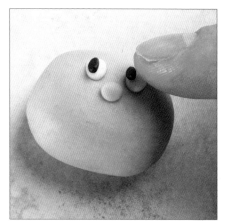

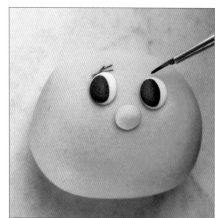

29 Mix white, teddy bear brown and flesh tone sugarpaste. Roll a ball into an oval for the head (check the size against the figure) and flatten it a little. Add a little ball for the nose and flatten it. Push in eye sockets with the bone tool.

30 Make the eyes with little white balls then smaller black balls for pupils. Wet the sockets and stick in place.

31 Mix dark brown edible paste colour with vodka and use a 00 paintbrush to paint three lashes above each eye plus a line underneath to suggest the cheek shape.

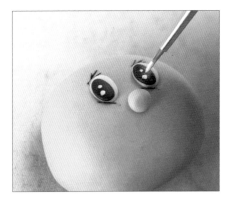

32 Use pearl white edible lustre powder mixed with vodka on the size 00 brush to paint on two little highlights in each eye.

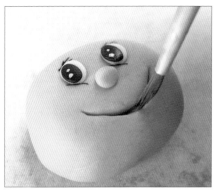

33 Cut the smile with a knife then wet a size 2 paintbrush and use it to soften open and stretch the mouth.

34 Use a smile tool to indent dimples in the cheeks.

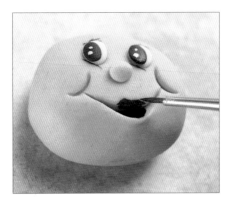

35 Paint the inside of the mouth with the size 00 paintbrush and dark brown edible paste colour with vodka, then paint the lips with red paste colour and vodka.

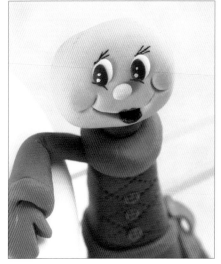

36 Dust the cheeks with rose edible powder food colour as for Santa (step 23, page 17). Push the head on to the spaghetti coming out of the neck.

37 Knead together yellow sugarpaste with half as much of the skin colour blend you used for the head. Push it through a garlic press to make hair.

38 Wet the head and place the strands of hair a few strands at a time, pressing them on gently with a tool. Create the hairstyle as shown. You can trim the ends.

39 Make earmuffs from a purple sausage and two flattened pink circles. Wet the hair and press them gently in place.

The boy figure

40 The boy has shoes like the girl figure (steps 18 and 19), legs like Santa (page 15, steps 1–5) in Atlantic blue and a top like Santa's in Lincoln green (pages 15–16, steps 9–12 but squarer and less cone-shaped) with patterns made with a quilting tool, and a hat like Santa's (page 17, step 28). His head is like the girl's (steps 29 to 35). His arms are like the girl's (steps 27 and 28) in Lincoln green with purple hands and no fur trim. His hair is made with long cones of chocolate brown sugarpaste and stuck on as for the girl figure.

41
Roll different sized balls of white sugarpaste for snowballs. Tip glitter into a food bag with the balls and shake together. Brush water on to the iced cake board and place the snowballs. Place the second arms on the figures and stick a snowball into each raised hand. Finish the cake by sprinkling some edible white crystal flakes around the snowman.

Details from the Snowball Fight cake.

Angel Cake

Stylish and eye-catching, this makes a beautiful wedding cake as well as a gorgeous centrepiece for the Christmas table. The stacking and carving techniques used here open up a whole range of potential designs and changing the way the wafer paper is cut will give an entirely different effect. This one is always much admired at wedding shows with its feathered effect suggesting an angel's wings and, displayed on a mirror with swarovski crystals, it is stunning.

You will need

Two 15.3cm (6in) and two 20.3cm (8in) round cakes

2kg (4lb 6oz) ganache

14 dowels

Wire cutters

Edible pen

Cake cards: 17.8cm (7in), 10cm (4in) and 7.6cm (3in) round

Cake boards: 28cm (11in) and 20.3cm (8in) round

Card, pen, scissors and sticky tape or 20.3cm (8in) high cone

Large serrated knife

Large palette knife

Turntable

2.5kg (5lb 8oz) white sugarpaste

Small knife

Rolling pin

Smoother

84 sheets edible wafer paper, 18 x 14cm (7 x 5½in)

800g (1lb 12oz) royal icing and piping bag

200g (7oz) white flower paste

Snowflake plunge cutters in 3 sizes

Edible glitter

26 gauge crimped silver wire

20 gauge wire

Circular mirror, 30.5cm (12in) in diameter

1 Level all the cakes and fill them with ganache. Push eight dowels through the bottom 20.3cm (8in) cake, 2.5cm (1in) from the edge, right down to the board. Start at 12, 6, 3 and 9 o'clock, then fill in the gaps, and add a dowel in the middle. Mark the dowels at the level the cake comes to with edible pen.

2 Take each dowel out and trim it to that level with wire cutters. You can sand the ends if they are wooden. Put the dowels back in the holes.

3 Spread ganache on the top of the cake to hide the dowels. Place a 17.8cm (7in) cake card on top and add ganache on top of this.

4 Place the second 20.3cm (8in) cake on top and then the 10cm (4in) cake card. Mark round this with a sharp tool. Push in the remaining lengths of dowel as before, in the middle and round the 10cm (4in) ring. Mark the height of the cake with edible pen, trim and replace as before.

5 Spread ganache on top to hide the dowels, then add the cake card and spread ganache on top.

6 Place one of the smaller cakes on top and mark round a 7.6cm (3in) cake card. As before, push in the remaining lengths of dowel in the middle and round the 7.6cm (3in) ring, mark and trim them to length and replace them, then place the final cake on top. Chill in the fridge.

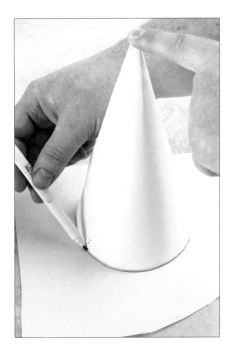

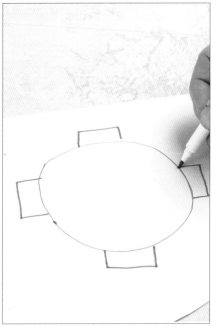

7 Use a 20.3cm (8in) ready-made cake cone or make one as follows. Cut a circle 40.6cm (16in) in diameter from card, cut it in half and fold and tape into a cone 20.3cm (8in) tall. Draw round the base on card.

8 Draw tabs as shown, cut out the base and stick it to the cone with sticky tape.

9 Place the stacked cakes on a turntable with the cone on top, ready for carving.

10 Dip a large knife in boiling water and begin carving, cutting an angle from the base of the cone to the base of the bottom cake. Keep wetting the knife so that it does not tear the cake.

11 Keep carving until you achieve an even cone shape, and then tidy up the edges.

12 Cover the layered whole cake and cone with ganache and chill.

The ganached cake.

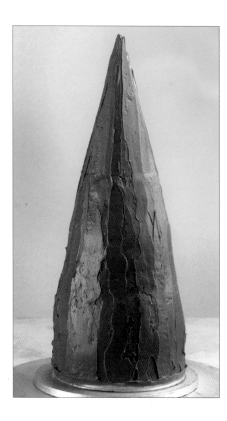

13 Smooth the chilled ganache with a palette knife dipped in hot water.

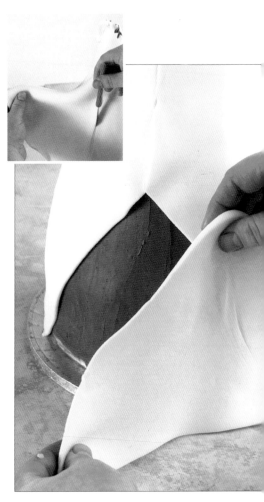

14 Roll out white sugarpaste, lift it on a rolling pin and and offer it up to the cake.

15 Flip the sugarpaste over the top of the cake and wrap it round.

16 Trim off the excess with a small knife to create a neat join. If there is a gap, create a patch to roughly the right size and shape and place this over it.

17 Trim to size to create neat joins. Smooth the sugarpaste with a smoother.

18 Cut triangles roughly 9cm (3½in high) and 4cm (1½in) wide at the base from sixty-four of the sheets of edible wafer paper. I do this by eye. Cut smaller ones 6.3cm (2½in high) and 2.5cm (1in) wide at the base from the remaining twenty sheets.

19 Use a piping bag to pipe a line of royal icing at the base of each triangle.

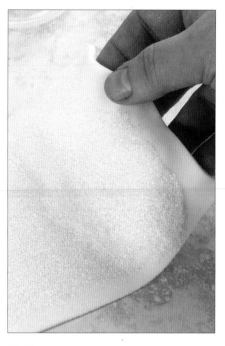

20 Stick the smaller triangles from the top, overlapping, until about 7.6cm (3in) down, then begin sticking on the larger triangles as shown. Cover the whole cake.

21 Roll out white flower paste and sprinkle it with edible glitter. Tip up the flower paste sheet to spread the glitter evenly.

22 Tip the excess back in the glitter pot. Use a snowflake plunge cutter to cut out snowflakes. Push down, wiggle, then push the plunger. Remove the snowflake from the cutter by pushing with your thumb. Make three sizes and leave them to dry overnight.

23 Where you are going to stick on a snowflake, first stick back the feather triangle with royal icing, so that it isn't weighed down. Stick on the snowflake with royal icing.

24 Allow two hours for the cake to set, then place it on a circular mirror for display. Decorate it with coils of crimped 26 gauge silver wire, hooked over the feathers. Place more snowflakes on the mirror. To make the star on top, feed 20 gauge wire through a big snowflake.

A detail from the finished cake.

White Chocolate Ruffle

You can almost smell the chocolate just by looking at this beautiful cake. Here modelling chocolate is stretched to its flexible limit to create this mouth-watering design. This is perfect for the chocoholic, with all the decorations made from chocolate too. You can use milk, dark or white chocolate and even a mix of all three throughout the cake. This version would be perfect for a winter wedding or for Christmas, but the cake can also be dressed in summer fruits to make a delicious seasonal variation.

You will need

Two 15.3cm (6in) and two 20.3cm (8in) round cakes

2kg (4lb 6oz) white chocolate ganache

14 dowels

Wire cutters

Edible pen

Cake cards: 17.8cm (7in), 10cm (4in) and 7.6cm (3in) round

Cake boards: 30.5cm (12in) round

Card, pen and sticky tape or 20.3cm (8in) high cone

Large serrated knife

Large palette knife

Turntable

1.5kg (3lb 5oz) white modelling chocolate

Rolling pin

Icing sugar

Pasta maker (optional)

Impression mat

Smoother

Small knife

Small circle cutter

Quilting tool

Ball tool

Sponge pad

Paintbrush

15mm (5/8in) white ribbon and non-toxic glue stick

Edible lustre powder in pastel gold and pearl white

Pearl white ediblel lustre spray

Spaghetti

1 Construct the cake as for the Angel Cake (see page 32) up to step 12, but use white chocolate ganache. The ganache does not need to be smoothed, as it will be covered with ruffles.

2 Warm the modelling chocolate ten seconds at a time in the microwave and roll it out to as thin as is manageable. Alternatively, put it through a pasta maker.

3 Cut the rolled out piece into 7.6cm (3in) wide strips, 15cm (6in) long.

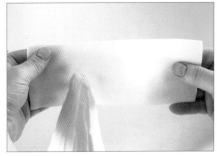

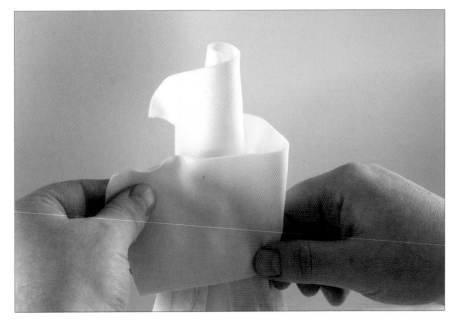

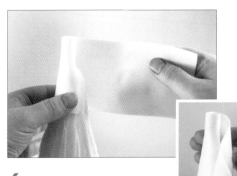

4 Sprinkle lots of icing sugar on the work surface and roll the strips out even thinner, to around 22.8cm (9in) long. A pasta maker is helpful here but is not essential.

5 Wipe the strip with your hand to remove the icing sugar. Offer it up to the cake so that the top of the cone is one-third of the way in and halfway up the strip.

6 Wrap the strip around the top of the cone, like a helter-skelter going down. Curl back the end to complete the ruffle.

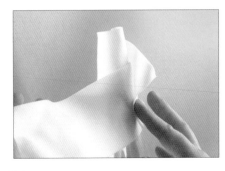

7 Take another strip and tuck the end inside the end of the first one. Wrap the ruffle round, halfway down the first one and press it down.

8 Pinch the ruffle at the bottom. This creates a ripple effect at the top.

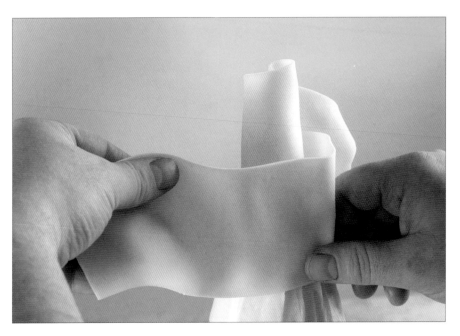

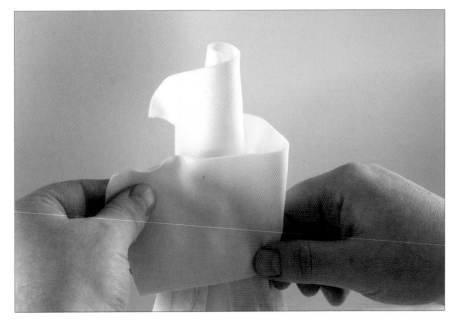

9 Continue, turning the cake on the turntable as you go and wrapping the ruffle round.

10 Place the third ruffle in the same way, tucking the end inside the end of the second ruffle and continuing round and down the cone, pinching and pressing it in place.

11 Texture the next strip with an impression mat. Sprinkle icing sugar on the work surface and on the strip, then put the impression mat on top and press it with a smoother (this gives less pressure than a rolling pin and will not damage the strip).

12 Place the patterned ruffle in the same way as the previous ones. As you continue down, alternate plain and patterned ruffles. If you cannot tuck in a new ruffle, you can attach it with a little ganache. Continue to the bottom of the cake.

13 Roll out more white modelling chocolate thinly. Cut out leaf shapes. I do this freehand.

14 Cut into the edges of the leaf shapes with a small circle cutter to make holly.

15 Indent lines with a quilting tool.

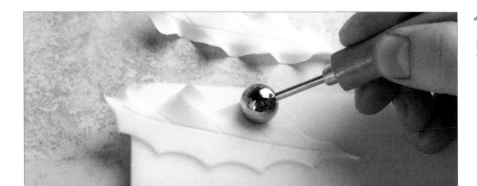

16 Place the holly on a sponge pad. Roll a ball tool over the edges to curl them into a holly leaf shape.

17 Paint the holly leaves with pearl white and pastel gold edible lustre powder, using a paintbrush.

18 Make fifteen roses with modelling chocolate as shown on page 19. Paint some with pearl white and some with pastel gold lustre powder.

19 Before attaching a rose, cut off the back with a small knife. Spread white chocolate ganache on the back.

20 Find a big gap in the wrapped ruffle design of the cake and place the rose carefully, wiggling it on. Place all the roses in the same way, then attach the holly with ganache, placing it carefully to enhance the overall design of the cake.

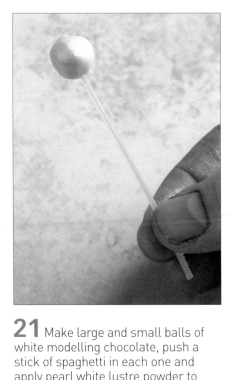

21 Make large and small balls of white modelling chocolate, push a stick of spaghetti in each one and apply pearl white lustre powder to the small ones and pastel gold to the large ones.

22 Push the spaghetti sticks into the cake to display the balls.

23 Roll out modelling chocolate thinly and cut it into rectangles, 5 x 3.8cm (2 x 1½in). Decorate the cake board with them, overlapping and hanging over the edge slightly. Tuck the last one under the first.

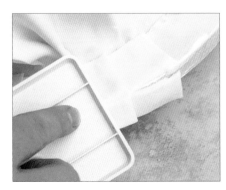

24 Trim at the edges of the board with a smoother rather than a knife, to get a smooth edge.

25 Decorate the cake board with a ribbon, then spray the cake with pearl white edible lustre spray.

Details from the White Chocolate Ruffle Cake.

44

Teddy Bear Cake

Who can resist this teddy bear cake? Cut out the shapes from the cake using the templates available at the end of this book, then simply stack them together and add fur in buttercream with a star piping nozzle. This design is very flexible and can be personalised in so many ways that it makes it a great design for any occasion, loved by adults and children alike. People always ask when they see this cake: 'How do you cut it?' to which we reply: 'Not in front of the children!'

You will need

25.4cm (10in) square cake

Large serrated knife

Cake cards: 30.5cm (12in) and 20.3cm (8in) round

Cake board: 30.5cm (12in) round

1kg (2lb 3oz) ganache

Palette knife

Dowel

Edible pen

Wire cutters

Sugarpaste:1.25kg (2lb 12oz) teddy bear brown, 750g (1lb 10oz) red and 250g (8½oz) each of dark brown, white, bright blue, Lincoln green and black

Rolling pin

Smoother

Red and white gingham ribbon and non-toxic glue stick

Small knife

Dresden tool

Large oval cutter

Large rose petal cutter

1.5kg (3lb 5oz) buttercream coloured with brown food colouring

Piping bag with no. 6 star nozzle and no. 1.5 plain nozzle

Red royal icing

Small holly plunge cutter

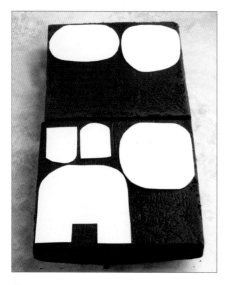

1 Cut a 25.4cm (10in) square cake in half. Make card templates from the templates at the end of this book and place them on the cake.

2 Carve out the shapes with a large knife. Cut two feet, one base piece with legs and one body. Carve two head shapes, plus an extra one half the depth of the others.

3 Place the body piece on top of the base piece with legs, then cut the right leg off as shown, carving round the body shape, so that you can move its position and it sticks out to the side rather than forwards.

4 Once the right leg is in its new position, carve both legs to round them.

5 Carve the body to round it. Begin with the knife flat on top, then curve downwards.

The cake with one leg and the top rounded off.

6 Pile up the three head pieces and round them off by carving.

7 Carve round to the base as well. Do not turn the head upside down as it will rock.

8 Once you have finished carving, massage the cake with your hands to perfect the rounded shape.

9 Carve the feet to round them. They bend outwards at an angle to the board, so carve the heel ends diagonally.

10 Place the feet on the legs as shown.

11 Lift the base parts of the cake on to a cake card and draw round it, then cut out the shape.

12 Put a little ganache on a temporary cake card and stick the cut-out cake card shape on top, then assemble the teddy bear base on top of this, sticking the pieces together with ganache.

13 Ganache over the whole body. There is no need to be neat at this stage. Put on the bottom slice of the head and spread ganache over the top.

14 Add the next slice of the head, spread with ganache and then add the top of the head. Push a dowel right through to the base, then lift it up 2.5cm (1in), as the cake will sink, and mark the level with edible pen. Take out the dowel and trim it where marked using wire cutters.

15 Coat the head with ganache.

17 Gently press the sugarpaste on to the cake. Tuck it between the legs, taking care not to tear it. Smooth it with your hands. If any large pleats form, press them together and trim them off with a small knife.

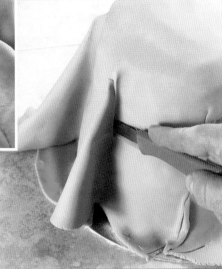

16 Roll out teddy bear brown sugarpaste to a piece large enough to cover the whole cake, and around 3mm (⅛in) thick. Pick it up on a large rolling pin and offer it up, then drape it over the whole cake.

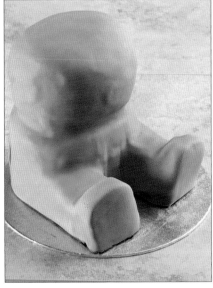

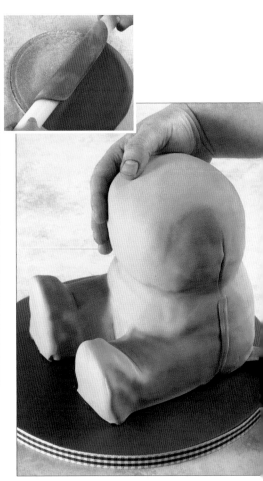

18 Press together the cut edges to join them neatly.

19 Continue smoothing the teddy bear shape with your hands and with a smoother to disguise any joins and to create a neat surface.

20 Ice a 30.5cm (12in) round cake board with red sugarpaste and trim with a gingham ribbon. Lift the cake on its shaped cake card off the temporary board and on to the iced board.

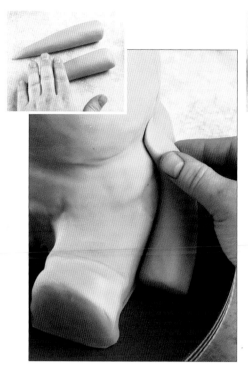

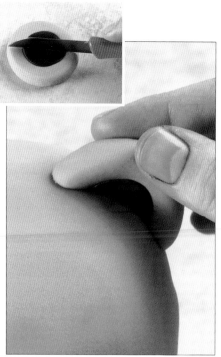

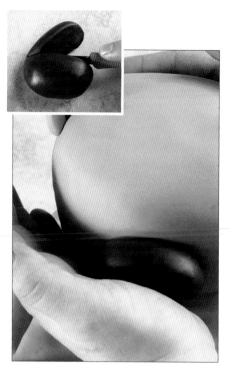

21 Wet the areas of the bear where the arms will go so that they become tacky. Roll two large tapered sausages in teddy bear brown sugarpaste. Try them for size, cut them to length at the paw end and attach to the bear.

22 For the ears, make a ball of teddy bear brown sugarpaste and flatten it a little. Make and flatten a ball of dark brown sugarpaste and press this on to the other circle. Cut in half to make two ears. Wet the teddy bear's head and push on the ears.

23 Make a ball of dark brown sugarpaste for the muzzle, roll it to a slight oval shape, then cut off the back third. Wet the teddy bear's face, then push the muzzle on, holding the back of his head with your other hand.

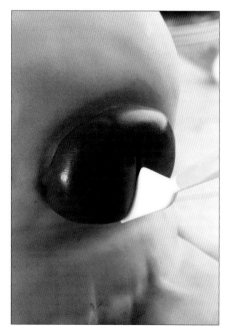

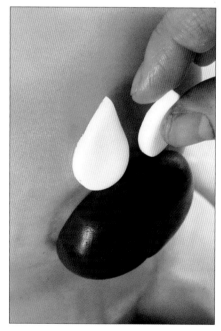

24 Mark a line from the middle of the muzzle down to the bottom with the Dresden tool.

25 Roll out dark brown sugarpaste and cut out two oval shapes. Stick these on to the feet for footpads.

26 Roll out white sugarpaste to 4mm (1/8in) thick and cut two eyes with a large rose petal cutter. Brush water on the teddy bear's face and stick on the eyes above the muzzle.

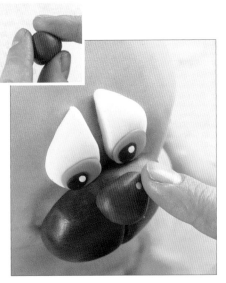

27 Make little balls of bright blue sugarpaste, roll them flat, wet the eyes and press on the blue circles.

28 Smooth in the blue circles with your fingers, then roll and flatten little balls of black sugarpaste and stick these on for pupils.

29 Roll a small ball of red sugarpaste, squeeze it into a slightly triangular shape. Cut off the back and stick the nose to the muzzle. Add tiny dots of white to the eye pupils and the nose for highlights.

30 Make buttercream with brown food colouring and use a piping bag with a no. 6 star nozzle to pipe fur. Start between the legs as this is the most awkward place, then under the muzzle and round the eyes, and round the footpads.

31 Pipe a row of flat fur in front of the ears, then pipe the rest of the ears in the usual way. After this, fill in all the rest of the teddy bear with piping, making sure you do not pipe in a pattern but keep it random.

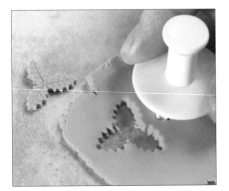

32 Roll out Lincoln green sugarpaste and use a plunge cutter to cut holly decorations. Using a 1.5 plain nozzle, pipe three dots of red royal icing on to the holly for berries, and add stitching details on the pads in the same way. Make the hat as for Santa (page 17, step 28) but larger. Add the holly decorations to the hat and the iced cake board.

Details from the Teddy Bear Cake.

Penguins' Igloo

Penguins and their antics bring this cake to life. They are easy to make (see page 18) and you can vary their positions and expressions in so many ways to suit your own ideas and sense of humour. The igloo is easy to carve and the brickwork effect is added to the sugarpaste covering with simple tools. Royal icing icicles complete the polar scene and there are snowballs to add to the penguin mayhem.

You will need

Two 15.3cm (6in) round cakes
Large knife
700g (1lb 8½oz) ganache
Palette knife
25.4cm (10in) cake card, round
25.4cm (10in) cake board, round
Pastry brush
Sugarpaste: 750g (1lb 10oz) white,
400g (14oz) duck-egg blue,
500g (1lb 1½oz) black and
250g (8½oz) orange
Rolling pin
Smoother
Ruler
Turntable
Dresden tool
Bone tool
Silver ribbon
Non-toxic glue stick
Diamante strip
Piping bag
Royal icing
Edible glitter and food bag

1 Level off both cakes and put one on top of the other. Carve into an igloo shape by rounding off the top cake with a large knife.

2 Cut the bottom cake in half and ganache inside. Draw round the cake on a 25.4cm (10in) cake card, adding a tab shape for the porch. Cut out this shape, put the cake on it and place on a temporary cake board. Use ganache to join the two cakes together, then ganache the outside.

3 Take a block of white sugarpaste and use it straight from the packet, without kneading it first. Carve it into shape to make the porch for the igloo.

4 Push the porch into place on the igloo.

5 Cut a thick strip of white sugarpaste. Wet the front of the porch and stick the strip on, making an arched shape.

6 Smooth the ganache with a pastry brush and boiling water. Roll out white sugarpaste to around 5mm (¼in) thick and large enough to go over the whole igloo with some to spare. Lift on the rolling pin and place it over the igloo.

7 Smooth the sugarpaste into the igloo with your hands and mark the base with the edge of the smoother, then cut off the excess.

8 Mould the sugarpaste around the door with your fingers, pushing it slightly into the indent.

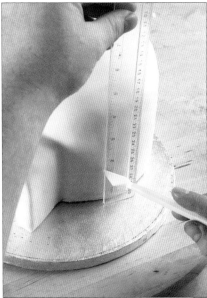

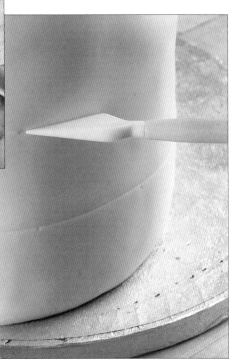

9 Measure 3.8cm (1½in) up from the base of the cake and mark with a Dresden tool. Turn the cake on the turntable and keep marking the same height, then turn the cake again and join all the marks to create the lowest bricks of the igloo. Continue marking the rows of bricks the same distance apart up the cake.

10 Continue going round the cake marking the rows of bricksuntil you reach the top of the igloo.

11 Mark the uprights of the brickwork, creating bricks 5cm (2in) wide. Mark the porch with brickwork in the same way.

12 Wet the end of a bone tool and run it along all the cracks to soften and widen them.

13 Roll out duck-egg blue sugarpaste to 4mm (¹⁄₈in) thick and ice and trim a 25.4cm (10in) cake board. Stick on a silver ribbon, then a diamante strip on top.

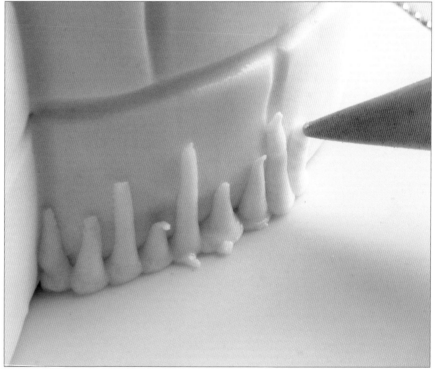

14 Transfer the cake on its cake card to the iced board. Pipe royal icing icicles up the side to different heights as shown. To add snowballs, roll balls of white sugarpaste. Tip edible glitter into a food bag with the balls and shake together. Brush water on to the iced board, the igloo and some of the penguin's flippers and place the snowballs.

Details from the Penguins' Igloo cake.

Santa's Face

Here is Santa looking very flushed after all his efforts delivering the presents. This is a good design for honing your skills at carving, covering and moulding a cake with an uneven surface. We are often asked for moulded faces and they can be tricky, but this one is a good place to start, as Santa's big features make it easier to get right. People will be reluctant to cut into Santa, but just remind them that he is delicious as well as looking great!

You will need

25.4cm (10in) round cake

Large serrated knife

800g (1lb 12oz) ganache

Palette knife

Sugarpaste: 600g (1lb 5oz) bottle green, 500g (1lb 1½oz) white, 400g (14oz) teddy bear brown, 300g (10½oz) red and a little black

Rolling pin

Small knife

Cake board: 35.5cm (14in) round

Smoother

Red ribbon

Non-toxic glue stick

Large and small circle cutter

Rose edible powder food colour

Paintbrush

Quilting tool

Cone tool

Ball tool

White flower paste

Snowflake plunge cutter

Edible glitter

1 Take a 25.4cm (10in) round cake and use the template provided at the end of this book to cut off the sides with a large knife.

2 Take off the sides you have cut and put them at the bottom, then trim round the template so that the scraps create Santa's beard area.

3 Cut the cake in half and ganache the inside, then stick all the bits together with ganache, and use it to coat the outside.

4 Knead together white and teddy bear brown sugarpaste. Roll two large balls for Santa's cheeks and cut off the backs.

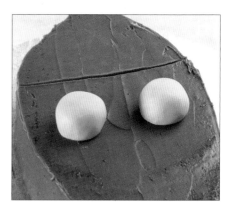

5 Mark the cake where the hat will go, put the cheeks in place.

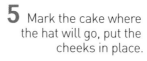

6 Roll out more of the same sugarpaste mix. Cut a wide band and place it over the cake, covering the cheeks.

7 Smooth the sugarpaste over the face with your hands.

8 Trim off the excess neatly at the top and bottom to allow room for the hat and the beard.

9 Roll out red sugarpaste, cut a straight line across it and lay it over the cake to make the hat, overlapping the skin area slightly.

10 Mark the hat sugarpaste at the base of the cake with a smoother, then trim off the excess. Cut a triangle from rolled out red sugarpaste for the hanging part of the hat, brush on water and stick the triangle on.

11 Roll out white sugarpaste, cut a straight line across it and place it over the beard area of the cake. Smooth with your hands.

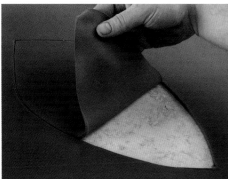

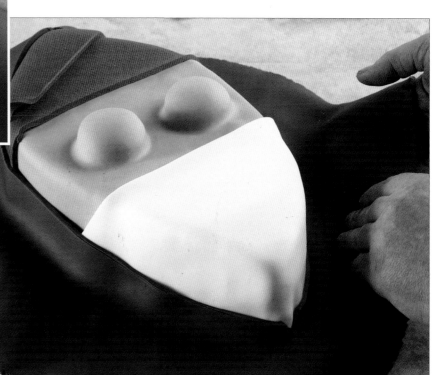

12 Roll out bottle green sugarpaste to 3mm (1/8in) and cut round the face template provided at the end of this book. Take out the middle piece. Place the remaining sugarpaste over the cake to ice the cake board. Smooth and push it in place against the cake. Trim the edges and stick a ribbon round the board.

13 Make a ball of the same skin colour as before and place this between the cheeks, checking the size first.

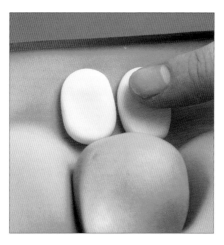

14 Make little white sausages of white sugarpaste and flatten them with your fingers for the eyes. Wet the face and press the eyes in place.

15 Roll tiny balls of black sugarpaste, brush water on the eyes and stick the pupils on.

16 Roll out skin-coloured sugarpaste and use a small circle cutter to cut out a circle. Cut this in half to make eyelids, moisten the eyes and stick the eyelids in place as shown.

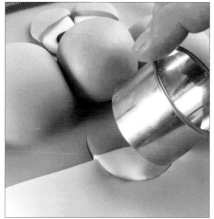

17 Use the bottom half of a large circle cutter to cut out Santa's smile from the top of the beard area.

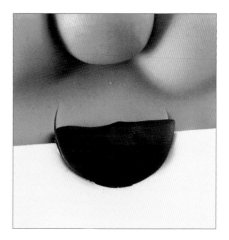

18 Cut a circle of black sugarpaste with the same cutter and cut it in half. Put in place for the dark inside the mouth.

19 Wet the area below the mouth. Roll a sausage of skin-coloured sugarpaste for the lower lip. Place it and trim the ends.

20 Wet the sides of the face. Roll out white sugarpaste, cut panels to fit the space between the hat and the beard, and press in place. Trim to fit.

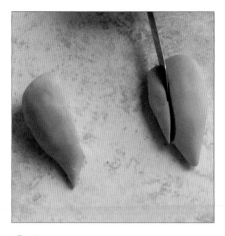

21 Make two large teardrop shapes from skin-coloured sugarpaste and cut off the sides to fit against the sides of the cake.

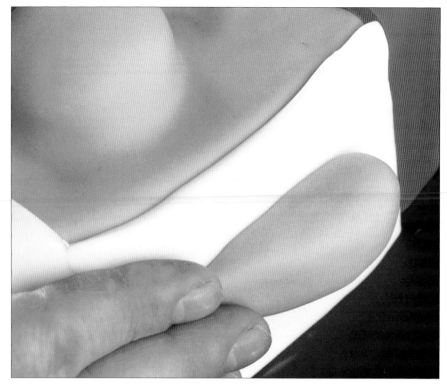

22 Brush water on the sides of the cake so that it goes tacky. Press on the ears.

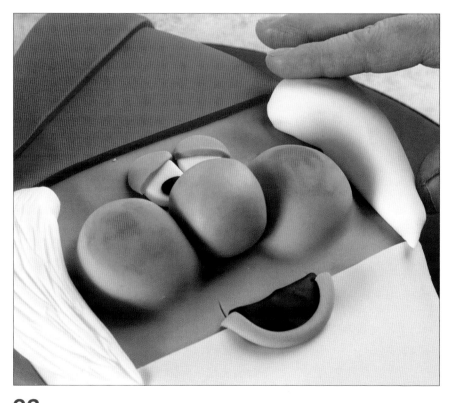

23 Dust the cheeks with rose edible powder food colour as for the smaller Santa on step 23 page 17. Make two tapered sausages of white sugarpaste for the hair, check for size and trim off the wider tops. Brush the face with water and stick on the hair.

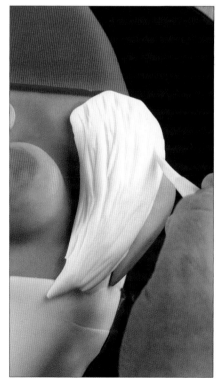

24 Texture with a quilting tool.

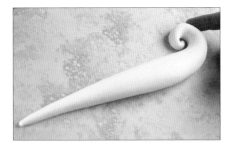

25 Make a large tapered sausage from white sugarpaste and curl both ends to make the moustache.

26 Place the moustache under the cheeks and nose, just ovelapping the mouth. Indent the centre with a cone tool.

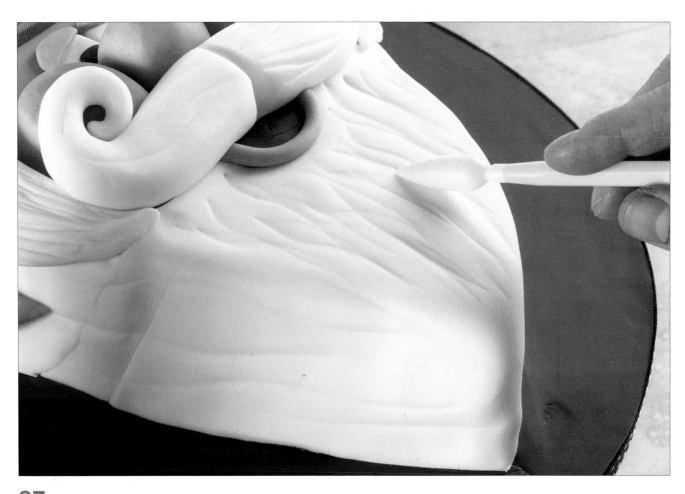

27 Use the cone tool to make wiggly lines on the beard, suggesting texture. Make the fur trim for the hat as for the small Santa (see page 15, steps 7 and 8), but larger! Decorate the iced board with snowflakes made as in steps 21 and 22 on page 37.

Details from the Santa's Face cake.

Christmas Wedding

Christmas wedding cakes are becoming ever more popular. This cake combines a contemporary wedding design with festive colours and decorations, but it can easily be adapted for a wedding at another time of year. The design pressed into the sugarpaste with an impression mat is highlighted by gorgeous bronze edible lustre spray, and the cake is festooned with sugarpaste ribbons and holly leaves, which could be replaced with different shaped leaves for an autumn wedding. We have displayed the cake on a specially made base surrounded with tasteful Christmas decorations.

You will need

Four round cakes: 25.4cm (10in), 20.3cm (8in), 15.3cm (6in) and 10cm (4in)

Large knife

2.2kg (4lb 13oz) ganache

Sugarpaste: 2.5kg (5lb 8oz) teddy bear brown and 800g (1lb 12oz) chocolate brown

Rolling pin

Small knife

Impression mat

Smoothers

Ruler

Turntable

Fourteen dowels

Cake board: 35.5 (14in) round

Cake cards: 20.3cm (8in), 15.2cm (6in) and 10cm (4in) round

Bronze edible lustre spray

Quilting tool

300g (10½oz) bulrush brown flower paste

Small circle cutter

Ball tool

Sponge mat

Edible lustre powders in sherry, gold and bronze

Paintbrush

Ribbon: 15mm (⅝in) wide gold and 10mm (⅜in) wide brown metallic

Non-toxic glue stick

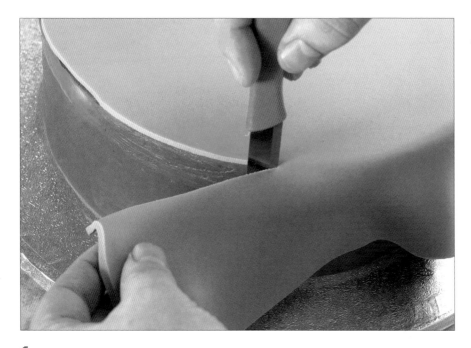

1 Make the four cakes and place the largest on a 35.5cm (14in) round board. Level them with a large knife, then fill and cover them with ganache. Roll teddy bear brown sugarpaste 3mm (⅛in) thick to cover the cake. Place it over the cake. Smooth the top with a smoother, then use a small knife to trim off the excess, leaving just the top iced.

2 Roll out and cut a strip of sugarpaste long enough to cover the sides and 8.8cm (3½in) wide. Wet the edge of the sugarpaste on the top of the cake so that it goes tacky. Place an impression mat over the strip and press with a smoother. Apply to the whole length, making sure you match up the pattern.

69

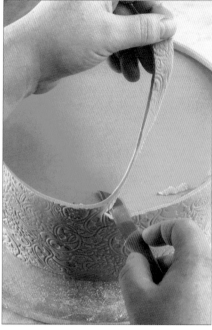

4 Trim off the excess at the top, pulling up the trimmed part so that you get a clean cut.

3 Wrap the patterned strip around the cake. Smooth it very gently with a smoother.

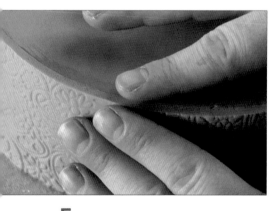

5 Put the cake on a turntable. Go round the cake, smoothing the join with your fingers.

6 Ice the cake board with the same sugarpaste, as shown on page 23. Attach a gold ribbon round the edge, then apply non-toxic glue stick and attach a second narrow metallic brown ribbon. Make the upper tiers of the cake in the same way. Insert dowels and cake cards to support their weight as shown in the Angel Cake steps 1 to 6 (pages 33–34.)

8 Make two long sausages of chocolate brown sugarpaste and twist them together to make a cord decoration.

7 Spray all four tiers with bronze edible lustre spray. The excess falls on the iced cake board and adds a sheen.

10 Roll out chocolate brown sugarpaste, cut out four strips for the bow and run a quilting tool down the edges. Cut out 'v' shapes from the ends of two of the strips. Press the ends of these two strips together to make two loops. Make a smaller strip in the same way but cut an inverted 'v' shape as shown.

9 Brush water around the bottom of the bottom cake and place the twisted cord around the base. Trim to fit.

11 Pinch the straight ends of the bow tails as shown to create the effect of a tied ribbon.

12 Brush water on the cake so that the bow will sit on the bottom tier, against the second tier. Place the bow tails and curl up the ends.

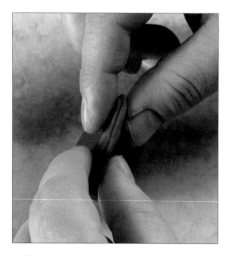

13 Take the loops and pinch the ends together.

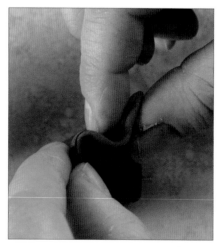

14 Push the flat edge of each loop into an 's' shape as shown.

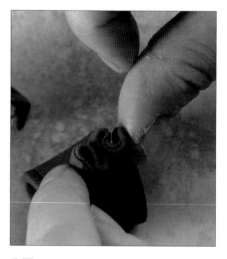

15 Push again to create a second 's' shape.

16 Trim each loop to the same size.

17 Brush water on to the second tier of the cake and stick on the first loop.

18 Place the second loop in the same way to create a neat bow.

19 Place the little centre piece to hide the joins and complete the bow.

20 Use flower paste in bulrush brown to make holly leaves as in the White Chocolate Ruffle cake steps 13–16, page 41. Use a paintbrush to dust them with edible lustre powders in royal gold, sherry and bronze.

21 Use the holly leaves to decorate all the tiers of the cake.

Opposite
Details from the Christmas Wedding cake.

End of Shift

This whimsical cake reflects that feeling we all have on Christmas Eve when everyone is in, the rush is over and we can relax. We can all empathise with poor, exhausted Santa here, but has he ever had to do a cake decorator's shift? This project calls upon your modelling and cake shaping and carving skills. Clear edible glaze spray transforms chocolate brown sugarpaste into armchair leather, and a knitwear impression mat creates carpet texture on the iced board. The fun of this cake is in the detail!

You will need

20.3cm (8in) round cake

Ruler

15.2cm (6in) round cake board

Two square cake boards, 25.4cm (10in) and 30.5cm (12in)

Large knife

450g (16oz) ganache

Palette knife

Sugarpaste: 250g (8½oz) black, 250g (8½oz) grey, 400g (14oz) red, 300g (10½oz) bottle green, 600g (1lb 5oz) chocolate brown and a small amount of yellow

Dresden tool

Rolling pin

Quilting tool

Silver edible paste colour

Knitwear effect impression mat

15mm (⅝in) spotted red and white ribbon

Non-toxic glue stick

Smoother

Pastry brush

Small knife

Cone tool

Coloured metallic balls

Clear edible glaze spray

Rose edible powder food colour

Paintbrush

Snowflake plunge cutter

Pearl white edible lustre powder

Food bag

Spaghetti

1 Take the cake and measure 14cm (5½in) across the diameter. Score a line at right angles to the diameter you measured and cut across the cake on the scored line to cut off one side.

2 Place the cut-off piece with the cut edge on the work surface and level off the top.

3 Place the cut-off piece on the main cake to form the back of the armchair.

4 Cut down through the edge of the armchair on both sides. The cut-off edges will form the arms of the armchair.

5 Trim the cut-off edges to fit and place them on the armchair to form the arms. Trim to form the armchair shape.

6 Place the armchair cake on a 15.2cm (6in) round cake board. Use ganache to join all the pieces, then coat entirely with ganache. Put in the fridge to chill.

7 Roll a sausage shape from black sugarpaste and cut it in half to form the boots. Use the Dresden tool to make a mark around the sides to create the sole.

8 Roll out some black sugarpaste and cut into two rectangles. Use the quilting tool to mark stitching along one edge of each.

9 Brush water on the tops of the boots at the back and attach the rectangles as shown, with the stitching at the top, to make the boot shape. Use the other end of the quilting tool to make the lace holes.

10 Make bows in black sugarpaste as for the Christmas Wedding cake (steps 10–19, pages 71–73), but without cutting 'v' shapes. Wet the fronts of the boots and stick on the bows.

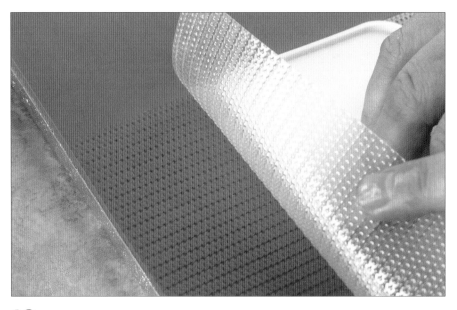

11 Make the foot spa by cutting a rectangular block from an unkneaded block of grey sugarpaste, straight from the packet. Indent a line around it with the quilting tool. Make a small sausage shape for the handle and push it on with the quilting tool. Paint the footspa silver with edible paste colour.

12 Ice two boards, a 30.5cm (12in) square with red sugarpaste and a 25.4cm (10in) square with bottle green. Use an impression mat with a knitwear texture to create the effect of a carpet on the board covered with red sugarpaste. Press with a smoother. Trim both boards with a spotted red and white ribbon, applied with non-toxic glue stick.

13 Smooth the chilled ganached cake with a palette knife and then a pastry brush dipped in hot water.

14 Roll out chocolate brown sugarpaste. Lift it over the armchair with a rolling pin, then smooth it in place. Make a little cut on the back of the seat area so that the sugarpaste does not tear. This will later be covered with a cushion.

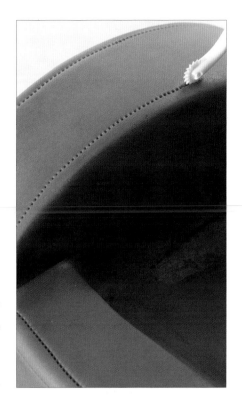

15 Mark the edges at the base with the smoother then trim off the excess with a small knife. Sharpen up the edges by pinching and smoothing. Run the quilting tool along the edges to create the effect of stitching.

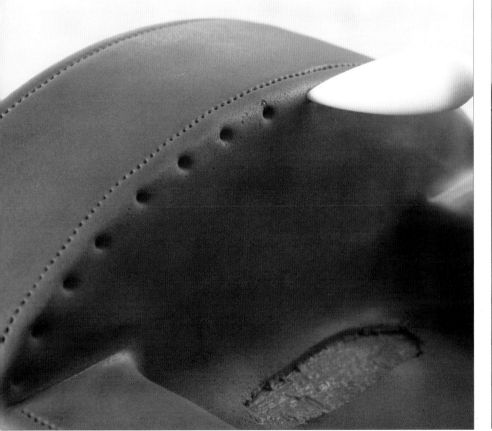

16 Make holes with the cone tool for the ball decorations. Brush the holes with water.

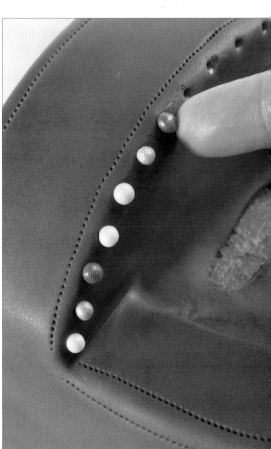

17 Push in coloured metallic balls to suggest rivets in a leather armchair.

18 Spray the whole armchair with a clear edible glaze for the leather effect.

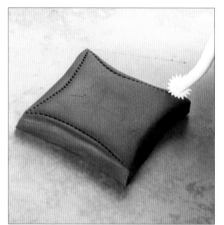

19 Roll bottle green sugarpaste to 8mm (5/16in) thick, cut into a 6cm (2³/8in) square and pinch the corners to make a cushion shape.

20 Mark the edges with the quilting tool to create stitching.

21 Roll out red sugarpaste, cut a snowflake with a plunge cutter, wet the cushion and press the snowflake on it. To make Santa, see pages 15–17. To make bubbles for his foot spa, roll balls of white sugarpaste. Tip pearl white edible lustre powder into a food bag with the balls and shake together. Brush water on the foot spa and carpet and stick on the bubbles. Add details like the sack to finish.

Opposite

Details from the End of Shift cake.

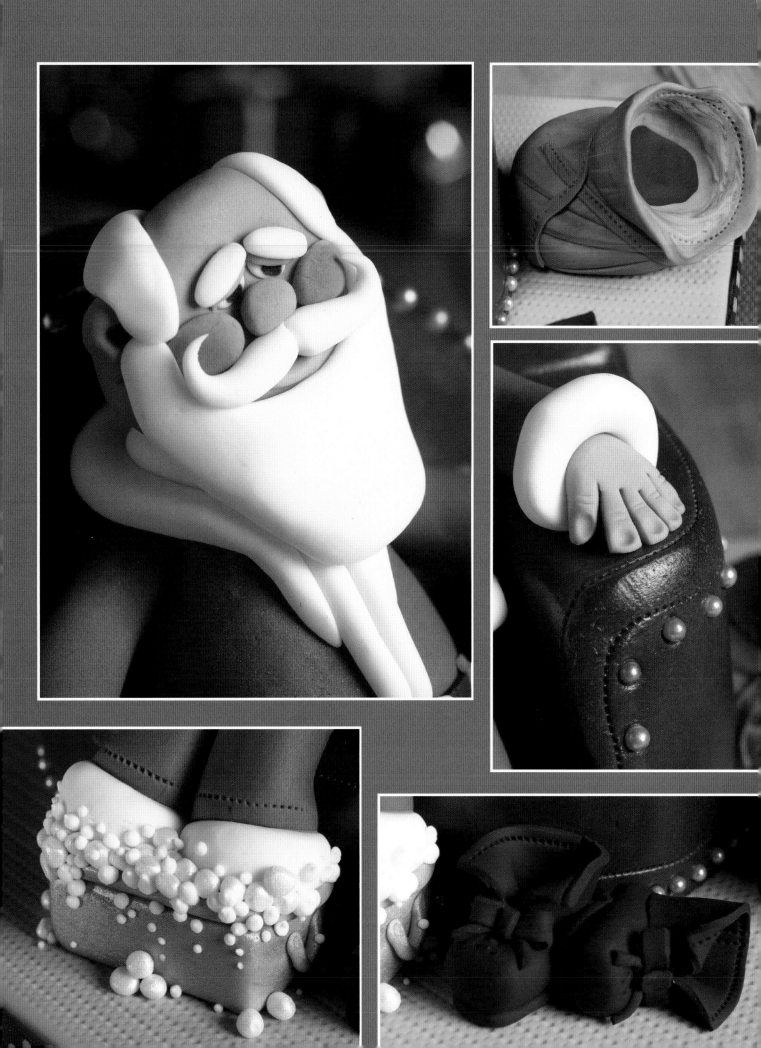

Santa Surprise!

This explosive cake certainly has the surprise factor! It features a topsy-turvy design created by carving the cake into a wedge shape, and contrasting stripes radiating from the centre. Once you have learned these techniques, you can use them for other cakes to create quite different effects (see the Topsy-Turvy Wedding Cake on page 92). This project has the additional fun element of figures bursting out of the middle of the cake.

1 Mark a line with the back of a large knife across the middle of the cake.

2 Cut a wedge from the side of the cake, one-third of the way down, to the top of the cake on the line you marked.

3 Flip the wedge you have cut over to the other side of the cake to create a sloping surface.

You will need

25.4cm (10in) round cake, 7.6cm (3in) deep

Large knife

700g (1lb 8½oz) ganache

Palette knife

25.4cm (10in) and 10cm (4in) round cake cards

35.6cm (14in) and 15.3cm (6in) round cake boards

Turntable

Metal scraper

Metal ruler

Pastry brush

Food bags

Sugarpaste: 800g (1lb 12oz) white, 400g (14oz) duck-egg blue, 400g (14oz) jade, 250g (8½oz) each of black, red, chocolate brown, teddy bear brown and small amounts of orange, yellow and green

Spaghetti

Rolling pin

Small knife

Two smoothers

Paintbrush

26 gauge silver wires

Snowflake plunge cutter

Non-toxic glitter

Pearl white edible lustre powder

15mm (⁵⁄₈in) wide green and white heart ribbon

Non-toxic glue stick

4 Cut the cake in half and fill with ganache to add height. Attach the wedge with ganache as well. Use ganache to stick a 25.4cm (10in) cake card to a temporary cake board and place the cake on top. Use ganache to stick a 15.3cm (6in) cake board to the the top of the cake to add height, offset towards the bottom of the slope.

5 Place the cake on the turntable. Wet a large knife in hot water and use it to carve the cake at an angle from the small cake board down to the board at the bottom.

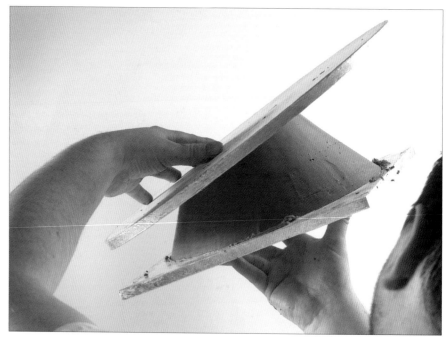

6 Coat the outside but not the top with ganache and smooth it with a metal scraper dipped in hot water. Trim off the excess ganache at the top and chill the cake in the fridge.

7 Slide a large knife dipped in hot water between the cake and the cake card to release it. Spread a little ganache on a (14in) round cake board, place it over the cake as shown and flip the whole thing over so that the cake is the other way up.

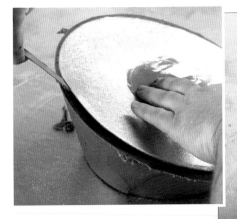

8 Remove the cake card carefully.

9 Cover the new top of the cake in ganache. Wet a metal ruler in hot water and use it to scrape along the top to smooth it. Smooth the edges with a palette knife, then brush the top with a pastry brush dipped in hot water.

10 Roll out white sugarpaste and place it over the cake. Make sure you catch the sugarpaste as it goes over the back rim of the cake and lay it down gently so that it does not tear. Massage the sugarpaste upwards with your hands to prevent cracks.

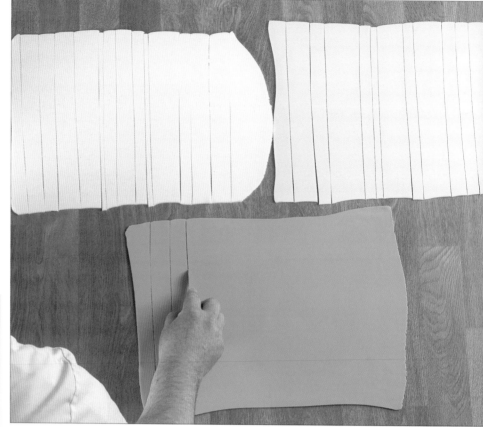

11 Turn the cake upside down on another board and smooth it. Tuck the ends of the sugarpaste under and trim the edge with a small knife. Turn the cake over again and use two smoothers together to sharpen the edges. Leave overnight to harden.

12 Roll out white, duck-egg blue and jade sugarpaste to exactly the same thickness: 3mm (¹⁄₈in), all together on one surface as shown. Cut off little strips of the different colours to compare the thickness until you have them all the same. Measure the cake from the centre of the top to the edge at the highest point and down the slope to the base: this is the length of strip you will need, so make sure all the colours allow for this length. Cover all the rolled out sugarpaste in food bags so that no air can get in and dry it out. Cut strips of different widths freehand from all the colours as shown.

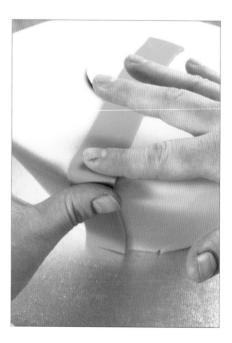

13 Roll out black sugarpaste and cut a 10cm (4in) diameter circle. Place it in the centre of the top of the cake and put a cake card of the same size on top.

14 Brush water from the centre of the cake to the edge at the highest point and down to the base. Take one of the coloured strips from under the protective food bags. Place it from the bottom, running up to the edge and along the top to the centre. Push it on from the bottom, making sure the edge is sharp.

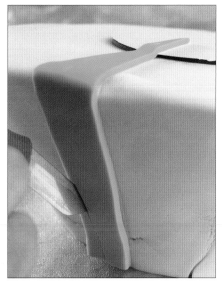

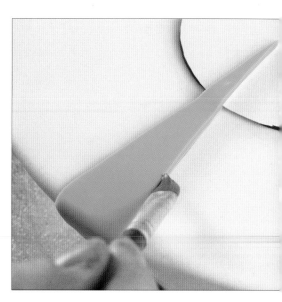

15 Trim to create a radiating stripe, coming to a point in the centre of the cake and at its widest on the edge.

16 Trim the part from the edge down to the base, narrowing a little towards the base.

17 Brush water on the edge of the strip.

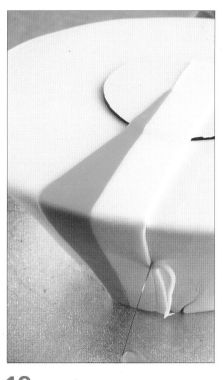

18 Butt the next strip up against the first as shown. Smooth it in place with your fingers so that the join is neat.

19 Trim off the excess to shape the strip in the same way as the first.

20 Peel off the excess to create another strip coming to a point in the centre.

21 Continue placing strips,
taking care to keep the sugarpaste covered with food bags while you work. Trim the strips as before and continue round the cake. Offer up the final radiating stripe and trim it carefully to fit against the first one.

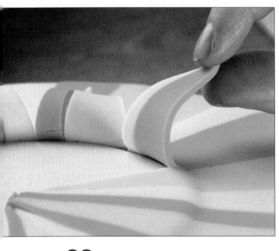

22 Peel back the stripes from the centre to create the exploding effect.

23 Release the cake card with a knife and take it off to reveal the black disk underneath. Ice the cake board with white sugarpaste. Make the top half of the Santa as on pages 15–17, using spaghetti sticks to strengthen his arms. Place this figure first. Make a reindeer top as shown on pages 121–123, but in chocolate brown sugarpaste with an added body and a teddy bear brown sugarpaste belly. Make the penguin as shown on page 18, but with yellow edging to his white belly. Wind 26 gauge wire round a pen to make the spirals. Push the ends into the backs of the figures. Decorate the board with snowflakes made with a plunge cutter, shaken in a food bag with non-toxic glitter. Add white sugarpaste balls shaken with pearl white edible lustre powder, and jade sugarpaste balls. Add a heart ribbon to the board using non-toxic glue stick.

Detail from the Santa Surprise! cake.

Topsy-Turvy Wedding Cake

This is a very contemporary design for a spectacular Christmas wedding cake that is well worth the challenge, as it never fails to surprise and delight people. Broken down into small steps it is very straightforward, and uses the same technique for making radiating stripes as the Santa Surprise! cake. The dark chocolate ganache really comes into its own here as a layering and covering material, as the topsy-turvy design would be very hard to pull off using buttercream.

You will need

15.3cm (6in), 20.3cm (8in) and 25.4cm (10in) round cakes, 7.6cm (3in) deep

Large serrated knife

1.6kg (3lb 8oz) ganache

Palette knife

Turntable

Metal scraper

Metal ruler

Pastry brush

Cone tool

Sugarpaste: 2kg (4lb 6oz) white and 500g (1lb 1½oz) grey

Rolling pin

Silver liquid paint

Paintbrush

Eight 20.3cm (8in) dowels and one 30.5cm (12in) dowel

Edible pen

Wire cutters

Cake cards: 7.6cm (3in), 12.7cm (5in), 15.3cm (6in) and 20.3cm (8in) round

Cake board: 30.5cm (12in) round

Edible white crystal flakes

Food bags

100g (3½oz) royal icing

Piping bag

Pearl white edible lustre powder

Silver balls

Non-toxic glitter

15mm (⁵⁄₈in) wide silver ribbon

Non-toxic glue stick

26 gauge crimped silver wire

1 Carve and ganache the cakes as for the Santa Surprise! cake (see page 84). Make a hole in the centre of the 7.6cm (3in) and 12.7cm (5in) cake cards. The 15.3cm (6in) cake will sit on the 7.6cm (3in) card and the 20.3cm (8in) cake on the 12.7cm (5in) card for stacking later.

2 Ice all the cakes with white sugarpaste as in steps 10 and 11 of the Santa Surprise! cake (pages 87–88), then leave to dry overnight. Decorate the bottom tier with grey and white stripes as for the Santa Surprise! cake (steps 14–19, pages 88–89), but do not pull them back. Leave to dry again then paint the grey stripes with silver paint. Ice the 30.5cm (12in) cake board with white sugarpaste.

To stack a topsy-turvy cake

3 Insert the 30.5cm (12in) dowel into the centre of the bottom tier. Measure 5cm (2in) out from the centre and insert eight dowels as shown on page 33. Place the middle tier on at the angle that it will sit on the cake below using royal icing to glue the tiers together. Repeat the process to place on the top tier. Place the stacked cake on the 30.5cm (12in) cake board iced with white sugarpaste and trimmed with a silver ribbon. Add the decorations as follows:

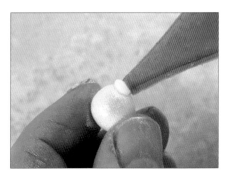

4 Brush a sugar and water solution over the middle 20.3cm (8in) tier and leave for fifteen minutes so it goes tacky all over. Tip edible white crystal flakes into a food bag, take handfuls and press them on to the cake.

5 Place balls of white sugarpaste in a food bag with pearl white edible powder lustre. Pipe a blob of royal icing on to a ball.

6 Push the balls on to the middle tier. The royal icing dissolves the flakes and the balls stick to the sugarpaste. Add more balls around the base of the bottom tier, alternating larger and smaller ones.

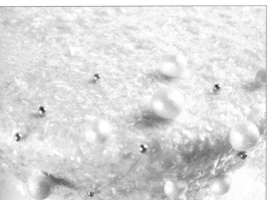

7 Attach silver balls with royal icing in the same way.

8 Make white roses as on page 19 and dip them in non-toxic glitter. Cut off the backs and attach them to all three tiers with royal icing. Finish the top tier with crimped silver wire. The decorations should be lifted off before the cake is eaten. Add silver balls to the top tier as well, surrounding the rose.

Details from the Topsy-Turvy Wedding Cake.

Gingerbread House

This is a gingerbread house with a difference, as it is made from chocolate cake and sugarpaste rather than gingerbread. It also has a Scandinavian stitched look that is very contemporary, while retaining traditional fairytale appeal. You can go to town with additional decorations of your choice. This cake will look amazing as the centrepiece on the Christmas table.

You will need

Two 25.4cm (10in) square cakes

Large serrated knife

1kg (2lb 3oz) ganache

Palette knife

Eight dowels

Black edible pen

Wire cutters

Cake boards: 11 x 15cm (4³/₈ x 5⁷/₈in) and 30.5cm (12in) square

Small knife

Sugarpaste: 250g (8½oz) red, 500g (1lb 1½oz) white, 900g (2lb) chocolate brown and 250g (8½oz) bottle green

Cone tool

Gingerbread man (or try it by hand) and small circle cutters

Spaghetti

Quilting tool

Pastry brush

Rolling pin

Straight-edged scallop cutter

Smoother

250g (8½oz) royal icing and piping bag

Stone wall impression mat

Blossom plunge cutter

15mm (⁵/₈in) red ribbon and non-toxic glue stick

1 Level off the cakes. Cut a 17.8 x 14cm (7 x 5½in) rectangle from each cake for the main part of the house. Place the two remaining large pieces on the work surface, one on top of the other, and the offcuts on top of these. All this will create the roof.

2 Carve from top to base in a triangle shape to create the roof.

3 Spread ganache between the two large pieces that make up the main house and place them on the 30.5cm (12in) cake board. Put a 11 x 15cm (4³/₈ x 5⁷/₈in) cake board on top and mark round it. Push a dowel through the cake inside each corner of the marked rectangle and another in the middle of each side as shown. Mark each dowel with an edible pen at the height at the cake and trim with wire cutters, then push the dowels back in.

4 Place the board back on top of the main part of the house over the dowels and cover it with ganache. Place the roof parts on top and ganache them all together. Cover the whole cake in ganache and put it in the fridge to chill.

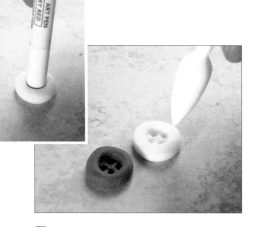

5 Make the various elements to decorate the cake while it chills. To make buttons, make balls of red and white sugarpaste. Flatten them and indent them with the end of a pen. Indent buttonholes with the cone tool.

6 To make candy cone trees, take one cone each from red and white sugarpaste.

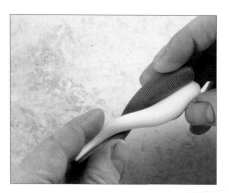

7 Twist them together.

8 Roll to smooth the cone.

9 Trim the wider end with a small knife.

10 To make a candy cane, place a long sausage of red sugarpaste and one of white side by side and twist them together.

11 Roll the cane to blend the colours. Curl the end over. Push in a stick of spaghetti to add strength.

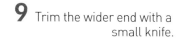

12 To make a swirl, roll a red sausage and a white one a little shorter. Place side by side. Curl over the end.

13 Push the curled part along to continue the curl and trim the ends.

14 To make a gingerbread man, cut a man out of rolled out chocolate brown sugarpaste. Cut two small circles of rolled out red sugarpaste using cutters. Place them side by side and use the gingerbread man cutter to cut into them as shown.

15 Remove the waste to reveal the red jacket pieces. Cut the ends of the arms to create the sleeve ends.

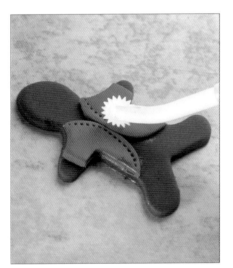

16 Place the jacket pieces on the gingerbread man, then mark stitching with the quilting tool.

17 Roll out bottle green sugarpaste. Cut out two tiny rectangles and cut 'v' shapes with a knife to create bow ties.

18 Make little balls of white sugarpaste for eyes, flatten them, dot the face with water and attach them. Add pupils and a smile with a black edible pen.

19 Make little circles of red sugarpaste for the cheeks and of green for the buttons to complete the gingerbread man.

20 Take the cake out of the fridge and smooth the ganache with a pastry brush dipped in hot water. Roll out chocolate brown sugarpaste and cut two rectangles 17.8 x 12.7cm (7 x 5in) for the side walls of the house. Smooth them on with a smoother.

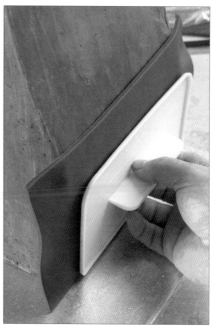

21 Trim the sugarpaste to size.

22 Cut two rectangles 35.5 x 22.8cm (14 x 9in) for the end walls of the house. Place these, smooth them and then trim them to size, creating the gable ends of the roof.

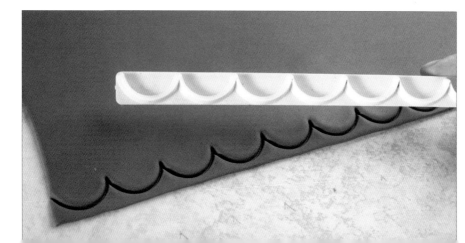

23 Cut a rolled out piece of chocolate brown sugarpaste with a straight-edged scallop cutter.

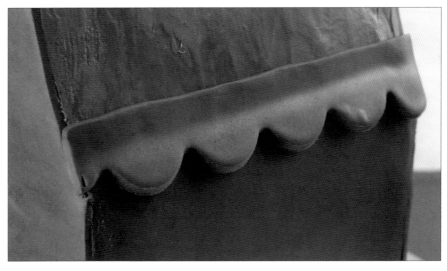

24 Measure 2.5cm (1in) up the edge of the sugarpaste and cut the scalloped strip to this width.

25 Brush water on the lower edge of the roof and stick on the strip.

26 Cut another strip in the same way and stick it on, overlapping the first as shown.

27 Continue up the roof until you reach the top and place the final layer along the roof ridge.

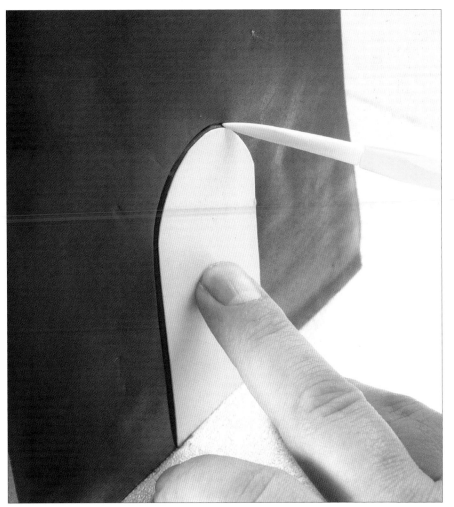

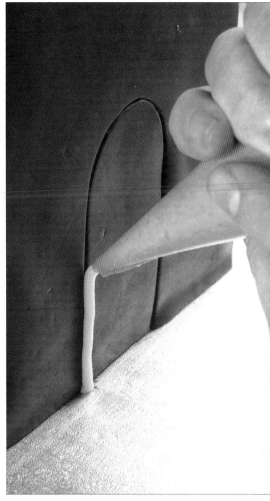

28 Use the arch template provided at the end of this book to make a card template for the door and mark round it on the end of the house with the other end of the quilting tool.

29 Pipe round the door with royal icing.

30 Cut rectangular blocks from an unkneaded block of chocolate brown sugarpaste. Stick spaghetti in as shown and leave to dry. Push in to the house over the door to create the gable of the porch.

31 Cut a rectangle for the chimney from an unkneaded block of chocolate brown sugarpaste. Cut at an angle to fit the roof as shown. Press the side with an impression mat to create the stone wall effect.

32 Press the other side and the front of the chimney in the same way. Attach to the roof using royal icing and add a chimney pot of chocolate brown sugarpaste rolled into a sausage and cut to size, with the end pinched out to hollow it.

Details from the finished Gingerbread House

Add the red and white punched flowers with dots of green sugarpaste for leaves. Make soft, runny royal icing and pipe it on for snow, allowing it to drip. Create the stitch effect by piping royal icing. Make balls of sugarpaste for the path. Ice the board by placing lumps of sugarpaste then draping a sheet of sugarpaste over the top. Make the shutters from 1.3 x 3.8cm (½in x 1½in) rectangles of chocolate brown sugarpaste and score them with a quilting tool. Pipe details with royal icing.

This page and opposite

Details from the Gingerbread House cake.

The Night Before Christmas

This cake is all about the detail in the decorations; the cake itself is the Christmas tree, and is relatively small. The fun is in creating the interior decor in the rug, fireplace and wooden floor, and the festive touches in the gifts, tree decorations, holly, poinsettia, stockings and wreath. Once you have mastered the techniques, you will have all the skills you need to create any number of beautiful cakes with finishing touches crafted in minute detail.

You will need

Sugarpaste: 400g (14oz) chocolate brown, 400g (14oz) teddy bear brown, 250g (8½oz) ivory, 350g (12oz) red, 250g (8½oz) black, 400g (14oz) bottle green and small amounts of orange and yellow

Rolling pin

Quilting tool

Two 30.5cm (12in) square cake boards

Black ribbon

Non-toxic glue stick

20.3cm (8in) and 15.3cm (6in) cake cards for drawing round

Holly plunge cutter

Edible lustre powder in pastel gold and red

Paintbrush

Large serrated knife

Dresden tool

Cone tool

Flower paste in bulrush, poinsettia and white

Smile tool

Smoother

Autumn leaf edible paste colour

Clear edible glaze spray

Blossom plunge cutter

Three 10cm (4in) round cakes

Circle cutters, 5cm (2in) and 3cm (1³/₁₆in)

200g (7oz) ganache

Scissors

Ball tool

Snowflake plunge cutter

20 gauge wire

Red non-toxic glitter

Gold balls

Tweezers

Royal icing and piping bag

Star plunge cutters

Gold liquid paint

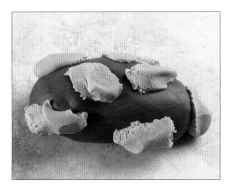

1 Take a large piece of chocolate brown sugarpaste and add blobs of teddy bear brown.

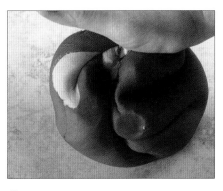

2 Knead two colours to create a marbled effect. Do not blend them entirely.

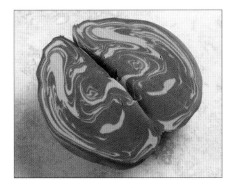

3 Cut the ball in half to check the marbled effect. You can blend it further if necessary. The marbled effect is used to suggest a wooden floor for the room.

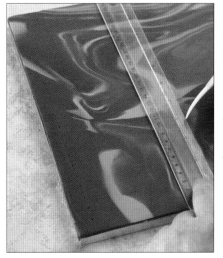

4 Roll out the sugarpaste, ice one of the square boards and smooth the edges with a smoother to trim them. At three points along the board, mark every 1.3cm (½in) along a ruler with a quilting tool.

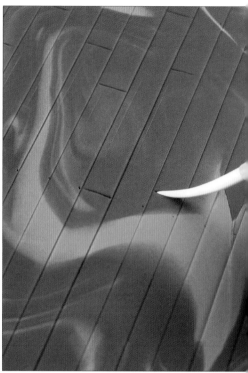

5 Join the marks you have made using the ruler and quilting tool, to create the effect of wooden floorboards.

6 Mark the ends of the floorboards in the same way. Indent dots for nails and decorate the edge of the board with black ribbon.

8 Lightly make a double row of stitching freehand.

7 Roll out ivory sugarpaste and cut out a 20.3cm (8in) circle to make the rug. Place it on the floorboard patterned board. Place a 15.3cm (6in) round cake board and card in the centre and go round it with a quilting tool to create the effect of stitching.

9 Take a holly plunge cutter apart and use the inside piece to print a holly pattern around the rug.

10 Dust the holly imprints with pastel gold edible lustre powder.

11 Press the end of the paintbrush into the ends of the holly leaves to create berries, then dust them with red edible lustre powder.

12 Fringe the edges of the rug with the sharp end of the quilting tool.

13 Use the stitching end of the quilting tool to add to the fringe pattern as shown.

14 Ice the second square cake board for the wall with red sugarpaste. Place a 2cm (¾in) trim of ivory sugarpaste at the top and indent halfway down with a knife.

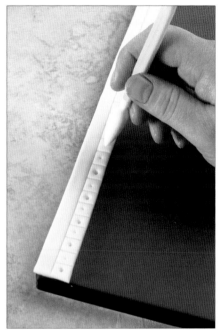

15 Indent little squares with the Dresden tool, then imprint dots with the cone tool, alternating between larger and smaller dots.

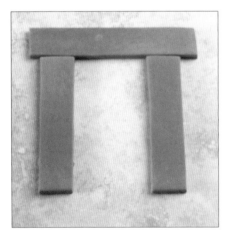

16 Roll out bulrush flower paste 5mm (¼in) thick and cut out three rectangles, one 13.5 x 3cm (5¼ x 1¼in) and two 16 x 3cm (6¼ x 1¼in) for the fireplace.

17 Use a smile tool to create a wavy pattern up the sides of the supports, turning the tool after each indent.

18 Add dots with the cone tool.

19 Indent the top of the top bar of the fireplace with two lines and a pattern wth the smile tool.

20 Roll out black sugarpaste and cut out a 7 x 13.5cm (2¾ x 5¼in) rectangle for the inside of the fireplace. Brush the red board with water first, then place the black piece in the middle allowing 0.5cm (¼in) at the bottom for the hearth. Square up with a smoother. Make two marks 1.5cm (⅝in) down from the top and 1.5cm (⅝in) in from the sides and indent lines from the top corners to these marks with the Dresden tool.

21 Indent an inner rectangle as shown, using the Dresden tool.

22 Brush water around the edges of the black rectangle and stick on the fireplace surround pieces as shown. Paint the surround with autumn leaf edible paste colour.

23 Spray clear edible glaze into the lid of the tin and use it to paint the black part of the fireplace, using a paintbrush.

24 For the flames, make seven red teardrop shapes, seven smaller orange and seven even smaller yellow ones. Press them all together as shown.

25 Cut across the bottoms of the flames and twist them a little with your fingers to get a lively, natural look. Press them on to the fireplace a shown.

26 Roll a long sausage of chocolate brown sugarpaste and texture it with the Dresden tool to create the effect of wood, then cut into two logs.

27 Place one log at the base of the fireplace. Cut the other one in half and place the two pieces as shown.

28 Roll out bottle green sugarpaste and rub pastel gold edible lustre powder into the surface. Cut out holly leaves with the plunge cutter.

29 Roll out thicker bottle green sugarpaste for the wreath and use 5cm (2in) and 3cm (1³/₁₆in) circle cutters to cut out a ring. Snip into the surface with scissors to create the effect of foliage.

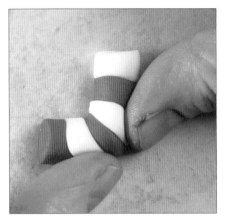

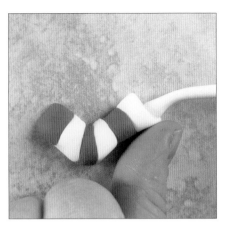

30 Roll a sausage in white and another in red sugarpaste. Cut them into sections and reassemble them as shown to make the Christmas stockings.

31 Bend the shape into a stocking and pinch the heel.

32 Indent the top of the stocking with a ball tool.

33 Punch flowers out of poinsettia red flower paste. Indent the centres, dot with water and stick on gold balls. Make candles by rolling tapered sausages of white sugarpaste.

34 Roll out poinsettia red flower paste and make a bow (see page 71). Spray with clear edible glaze, pick up with tweezers and dip in red non-toxic glitter.

35 The Christmas tree is made from three cakes 10cm (4in) in diameter, carved as for the Angel Cake (see page 35). Assemble it on a separate little board so that you can reach round it while working on it. You do not need dowels. Ice with bottle green sugarpaste in the same way as the Angel Cake. Make cones from the same sugarpaste and flatten them. Pull the Dresden tool over them to create texture, then leave them to dry in batches of ten.

36 Push the flattened cones on to the tree from the top, overlapping them as shown. Punch a snowflake with a plunge cutter in white flower paste and attach it to the top of the tree with 20 gauge wire. Decorate the tree with white royal icing dots, stars made using a star plunge cutter, ribbons and bows.

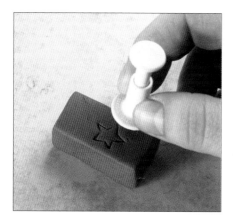

37 To make the gifts, cut the shapes from a solid block of red sugarpaste and punch impressions of stars in different sizes in the sides using the star plunge cutter. Paint with gold liquid paint. Make ribbons in contrasting colours and add bows on top.

White Out!

This hilarious design inspires many jokes about Santa having one too many glasses of the sherry or whiskey people leave out for him. The cake needs to be positioned so everyone can see the reindeer heads coming out the front of the snowdrift as well as the rumps sticking out of the back. Use the templates provided at the end of this book to create the sleigh from red flower paste, with plenty of ornate decoration worthy of this magical mode of transport. Once you have followed the steps to make the reindeer, you will be able to add these to other festive cakes by simply adding the hidden middle sections.

You will need

200g (7oz) red flower paste
25.4cm (10in) square cake
30.5cm (12in) square cake board
Large serrated knife
700g (1lb 8½oz) ganache
Palette knife
Sugarpaste: 1.5kg (3lb 5oz) white, 250g (8½oz) chocolate brown, 500g (1lb 1½oz) teddy bear brown, 250g (8½oz) red, 250g (8½oz) bottle green and small amounts of green and yellow
Rolling pin
Red stitch effect ribbon
Non-toxic glue stick
Paintbrush
Quilting tool
Small knife
Black edible pen
Spaghetti
Modelling chocolate
Scissors
Dresden tool
250g (8½oz) royal icing
Piping bag
Smoother
Food grade alcohol or vodka
Snowflake edible lustre powder
Gold liquid paint
3mm (⅛in) red ribbon for reins
Three dowels

1 Roll out red flower paste and use the templates provided at the end of this book to cut out all the pieces for the sleigh. Leave to dry overnight for assembly later.

2 Place a 25.5cm (10in) square cake upside down and mark it with a knife halfway across.

3 Cut from the central mark down to the bottom edge as shown.

4 Flip over the part you have cut off to create a wedge shape.

5 Cut a wedge shape off each side.

6 Carve the bottom of the slope to round off the corners.

7 Place the cake on the board at an angle and trim it to fit. Put the scraps on top to build up the height.

8 Attach all the pieces together with ganache, and cut the main cake in half and ganache the middle. Cover the whole cake with ganache. Wet the cake board with water. Roll out white sugarpaste and drape it over the cake with a rolling pin.

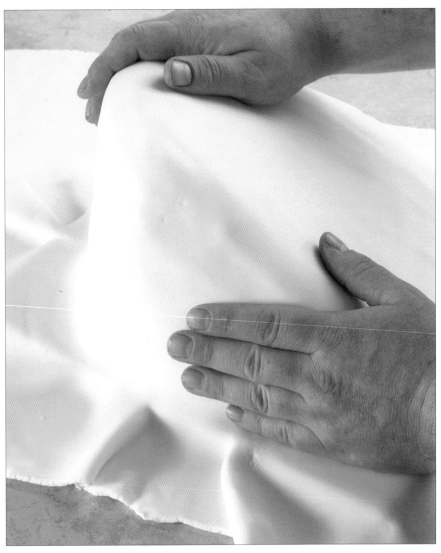

9 Smooth the sugarpaste over the cake and the board. Trim off the excess and add a ribbon to the board.

10 Knead together teddy bear brown and chocolate brown sugarpaste to make the reindeer colour. Make a cone for the head and roll under your finger to shape an indent.

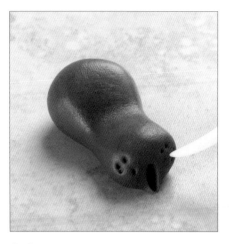

11 Indent the mouth with the end of a paintbrush and dot whiskers with the sharp end of the quilting tool.

12 Make little balls of white sugarpaste and flatten them. Stick them on for the eyes and dot with a black edible pen. Make a small circle of the reindeer colour, cut in half and place as eyelids.

13 Add eyebrows with the black edible pen.

14 Make little teardrops with the reindeer coloured sugarpaste for ears. Place them on the head then indent them with the quilting tool and flick up the ends.

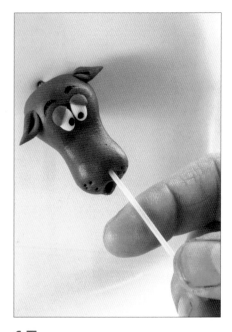

15 Push a stick of spaghetti through the head and stick it into the thick end of the cake wedge so that the reindeer is emerging from a bank of snow.

16 Make a ball of red sugarpaste and stick this on over the pasta to create Rudolph's nose. Make the antlers from two tapering sausages of modelling chocolate and snip into them with scissors. Wet the white sugarpaste above the head and push on the antlers.

17 Make the legs with sausages of the reindeer colour sugarpaste, and push spaghetti sticks through them. Make the hooves with a flattened teardrop shape and cut the indent in them. Push on to the legs and stick the spaghetti ends of the legs into the cake as shown.

18 The second reindeer is more deeply embedded in the snow so should be just muzzle, eyes and nose. Make the muzzle as before but cut off the back, and push it into the snow bank with spaghetti.

19 Add eyes and eyelids as for Rudolph, but make the nose brown and the legs shorter.

20 To make the reindeer's rear end, make a ball, cut off the back and stick it in place. Snip a tail with scissors.

21 Indent with the Dresden tool and score fur with the quilting tool.

22 Make legs and hooves as before and stick them in.

23 To make the tree, make a cone of bottle green sugarpaste and snip into it with scissors to create the effect of fir tree foliage.

24 Pipe royal icing in a piping bag to make impact marks in the snow around the reindeer.

25 Pipe royal icing around the reindeer's rear end as well.

26 Place the tree in the corner of the cake board and tip on snowflake edible lustre powder for snow.

27 The parts of the sleigh should be dry enough to use now. Pipe a line of royal icing along the sleigh as shown.

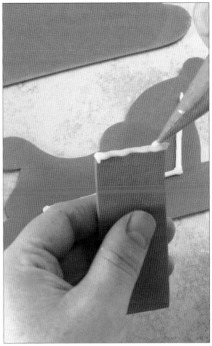

28 Pipe another line down the end of the longest rectangular piece.

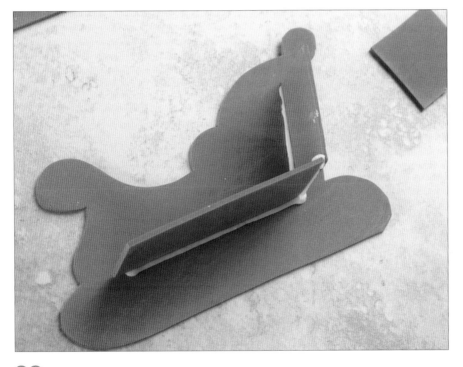

29 Place the longest piece and the next longest piece as shown to create the body of the sleigh.

30 Pipe royal icing at the other end of the longest rectangular piece.

31 Place the shortest rectangular piece as shown.

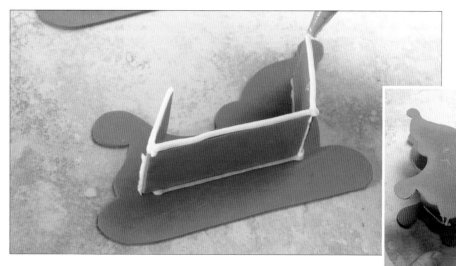

32 Pipe royal icing along the other edge of the sleigh body, then stick on the other side of the sleigh. Use a smoother to check the heights of all sides to make sure the sleigh is level.

33 Stand the sleigh up. Blend in the royal icing with clear food grade alcohol or vodka. Leave to dry, ideally overnight.

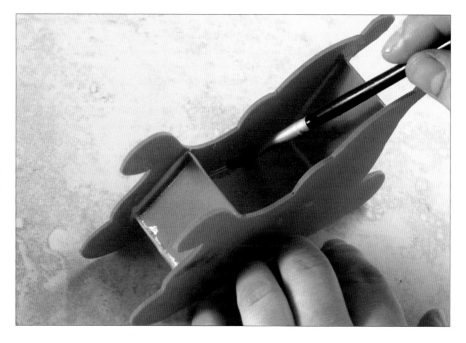

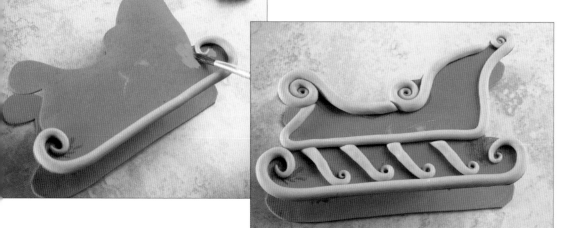

34 Brush the edges of the sleigh with water. Make thin, tapered sausages of teddy bear brown sugarpaste, place on the sleigh and curl the ends. Tease the curls into shape with the brush. Complete the decoration as shown and leave a day before painting.

35 Paint edible gold liquid paint on all the sleigh decorations.

36 Stick three dowels in the cake as shown to support the sleigh.

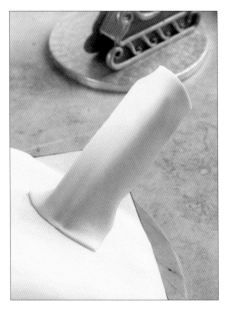

37 Cover the dowels in white sugarpaste and smooth it in.

38 Pipe royal icing on the covered dowels and place the sleigh on top.

39 Make Santa's sack with chocolate brown sugarpaste. Make a teardrop shape and pinch out the end. Put this in the back of the sleigh before the figure. Make Santa as on pages 15–17. Use thin red ribbon for reins. Push the ends into the snow and the other ends in Santa's hands.

This page and opposite

Details from the White Out! cake.

Christmas Down Under

This cake is ideal for someone who would love a high performance car for Christmas! It is far from traditional, showing Santa and his helpers enjoying an antipodean summer festive season. The car involves shaping, moulding and carving, as well as adding details.

Once you have learned how to make it, you can stage your convertible in any scene you like.

1 Cut a 14cm (5½in) wide rectangle from the 25.5cm (10in) square cake. Put the spare bits of cake at the back to form Santa's car.

2 Score lines to form a 10cm (4in) square to make the well of the car for the figures to sit in. This should be 16.5cm (6½in) along from the front of the car.

3 Take away the back end of the car and cut halfway down to make the sitting area.

You will need

25.5cm (10in) square cake
40.6cm (16in) square cake board
25.4cm (10in) square cake card
Large serrated knife
Cake card
Ganache
Palette knife
Pastry brush
Sugarpaste: 600g (1lb 5oz) grey, 500g (1lb 1½oz) teddy bear brown, 250g (8½oz) white, 500g (1lb 1½oz) black, 1.5kg (3lb 5oz) lime green, 250g (8½oz) red, 400g (14oz) chocolate brown, 250g (8½oz) yellow, 250g (8½oz) orange
Rolling pin
Small knife
Star nozzle
Black ribbon and non-toxic glue stick
Dresden tool
Circle cutters in 10cm (4in), 5cm (2in) and various smaller sizes
Smoother
Ruler
Bone tool
Two oval cutters
Quilting tool
Snowflake plunge cutter
Spaghetti
Smile tool
Two 20 gauge wires
Florist tape
Green flower paste
Edible powder food colour in forest green and apple green
Milk modelling chocolate
Silver edible paste colour
Tiny ball tool
Red and black edible pens
Blossom cutters
Rose edible powder food colour
Paintbrush

4 Cut away a piece of the same depth from the back end of the car to complete the sitting area.

5 Score lines from the sitting area to the front of the car, then carve the bonnet shape, tapering slightly towards the front.

6 Cut down at an angle to shape the area of the headlights.

7 Carve to round off the edges.

8 Shape the back of the car in the same way with lines tapering towards the back, carved as before. Round off the edges.

9 Cut the 25.4cm (10in) cake card to size for the car to sit on, spread on a little ganache and put the cake on top. Cut through the middle of the cake and ganache it, then coat the whole car with ganache.

10 Chill the cake in the fridge, then resmooth it with a palette knife and then a pastry brush dipped in hot water.

11 Roll out grey sugarpaste to cover a 40.6cm (16in) square board. Wet the board, place the piece in the middle of the board and then trim it to a 20.3cm (8in) strip of road.

12 For the sand at the sides of the road, roll out teddy bear brown sugarpaste and cut two pieces large enough to cover the edges of the board. Wet the board, place the pieces and trim them to size.

13 Use a star nozzle to add texture to the sugarpaste, suggesting sand. Put the nozzle on your finger and poke repeatedly into the sugarpaste.

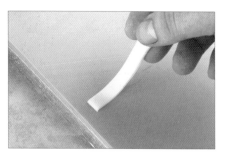

14 Make white sugarpaste strips for the road markings, brush the road surface and stick these on, wherever they will show beyond the car. Attach a black ribbon round the edges of the board.

15 Take the cake out of the fridge. Smooth again with a palette knife dipped in hot water. Reshape the bonnet detail by scoring with a Dresden tool, making a narrow mark first then turning the tool on its side as shown.

16 Brush with a pastry brush dipped in hot water to smooth the effect.

17 To make the wheel arches, roll out black sugarpaste 1cm (³⁄₈in) thick, cut a rectangle 10cm (4in) long and just under the height of the car. Push it on with a smoother where the wheel will go and carve it to shape with a knife.

18 Place and carve all four wheel arches in this way and use a smoother to smooth the edges. Use a 5cm (2in) circle cutter to hollow out the area for the wheel and pull the sugarpaste circles out.

19 Roll out thinner sugarpaste and cut out 5cm (2in) circles, then push these in to hide the cake inside the wheel arches.

20 Use a Dresden tool to cut into the wheel arches to create an arch shape instead of a circle. Push in scraps of sugarpaste to line the lower edges of the arch.

21 Make strip of black sugarpaste 2.5cm (1in) high to go round the base of the whole car and place it in patches as shown.

22 Roll out enough lime green sugarpaste to cover the whole car and lift it over the car on a rolling pin.

23 Smooth and shape the sugarpaste over the cake with your hands.

24 Cut a cross in the sugarpaste at the base of the well where the figures will sit, so that it doesn't tear. Shape the sugarpaste around the well with your fingers.

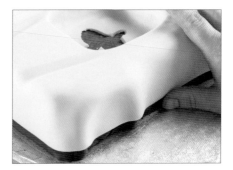

25 Go round the base of the car with a smoother to score the edge, then trim with a knife. Trim again to leave 1cm (³/₈in) of the black trim showing. Use your hands to soften the edge.

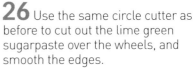

26 Use the same circle cutter as before to cut out the lime green sugarpaste over the wheels, and smooth the edges.

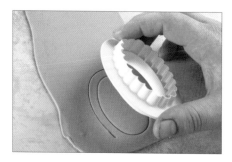

27 Use the Dresden tool to score marks for the doors and the trim at the bottom.

28 Use a bone tool to score the door handle indent.

29 Roll out grey sugarpaste very thin and cut with an oval cutter, then score with a smaller over cutter inside this to make the radiator.

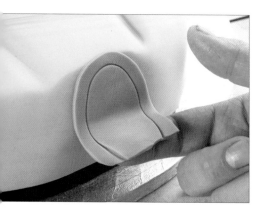

30 Brush the front of the car with water and stick on the radiator grille.

31 Use a ruler to help you score lines for the radiator grille with the back of a knife.

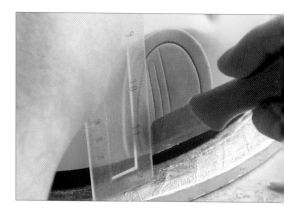

32 Trim the bottom of the radiator grille, brush water below it for the bumper and roll a long sausage of grey sugarpaste. Trim off the back and attach.

33 Make tiny balls of grey sugarpaste for indicators, flatten and attach them with a little water.

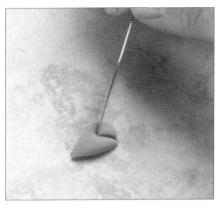

34 Make a little cone in grey sugarpaste, flatten it a little and cut out a 'v' shape as shown to make the decoration to go on the front of the car.

35 Place a small ball of grey sugarpaste over the radiator grille as shown and stick the decoration on top.

36 Use the template provided at the end of this book to cut out headlights from rolled out white sugarpaste and place them on the car.

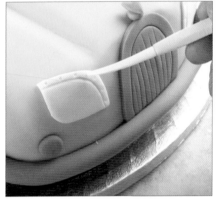

37 Add details with the quilting tool as shown: a row of dots and an indented line.

38 Make little sausages from grey sugarpaste and place these below the headlights, then make balls of red sugarpaste for the indicator lights.

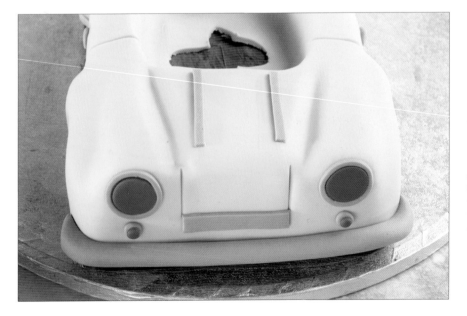

39 Use circle cutters in two sizes to cut grey rings for the rear light trims, and red circles for the lights themselves. Add a bumper and indicators as before. Place grey strips along the boot and for the rear registration plate. Add indentations either side with the Dresden tool.

40 Roll out black sugarpaste thickly and cut out four wheels with the 5cm (2in) circle cutter. Indent with the end of a small rolling pin.

41 Cut out a grey snowflake with a plunge cutter. Wet a tyre and place in the middle. Repeat for all four.

42 Make a grey ring with two circle cutters as before and add this to the tyre. Repeat for all four.

43 Use the Dresden tool to score lines for the tyre tread. Leave the wheels to dry for twelve hours.

44 Brush water in the wheel arches and attach the wheels.

45 Roll out black sugarpaste large enough to cover the well where the figures go. Push it in place and smooth it with your hands.

46 Trim away the excess with a small knife.

47 Roll out black sugarpaste to 4mm (¼in). Cut to 11.5 x 3.8cm (4½ x 1½in). Place it in the well of the car for the back seat. Indent it with the Dresden tool to create upholstery.

48 Roll black sugarpaste to 6mm (⁵/₁₆in) thick and cut two seats 3.8 x 5cm (1½ x 2in). Stick to the well floor with water and push in two short sticks of spaghetti.

49 Push on two small black ovals for headrests. Make a steering wheel in the same way as the wheel alloys: with a ring and a snowflake in grey sugarpaste.

50 Make lime green cones, flatten them, push sticks of spaghetti into them and push them in for wing mirrors.

51 Take an unkneaded block of chocolate brown sugarpaste and cut a small block 6 x 3.5cm (2³/₈ x 1³/₈in) and 2.5cm (1in) deep for the picnic basket. Indent it with the Dresden tool to suggest the lid and imprint dots with the other end of a smile tool for basketwork. Cut strips of teddy bear brown for the hinges and straps and indent them with the sharp end of the Dresden tool. Roll a tiny sausage for the handle and indent in the same way.

52 Roll a large tapered sausage from chocolate brown sugarpaste and cut it into sections for a palm tree trunk.

53 Take two 20 gauge wires and tape them together with florist tape, twisting it around them.

54 Feed the sections of the trunk on to the wires, slightly offset to create an irregular shape.

55 Trim off the top of the wires and add texture to the trunk by marking it with the other end of the Dresden tool.

56 Roll out green flower paste, cut into a leaf shape and use a knife to fringe the edges to make a palm frond. Make several fronds.

57 Wrap bits of wire in florist tape and place in the end of each frond. Dust the fronds with forest green and apple green edible powder food colour and push them into the trunk. Add a little ball of chocolate brown sugarpaste to hide the wires.

58 To make Rudolph's legs, make two teardrop shapes, flatten the narrow end and roll under your finger to indent.

59 To make the antlers, make two tapered sausages from modelling chocolate, flatten them a little and cut them as shown.

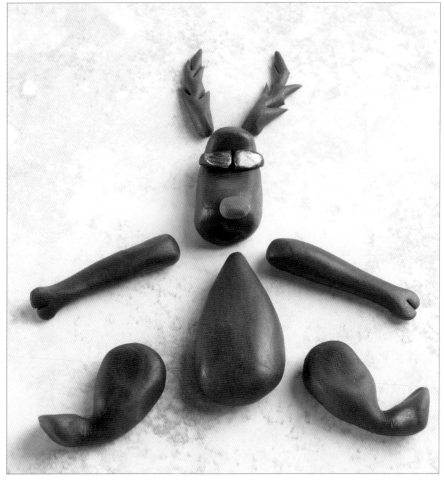

60 Make a cone from chocolate brown sugarpaste for the body. Make tapered sausages, indent a little for wrists and indent them with a knife to make hooves. Indent the leg hooves as well. Make the head from a cone, flattened a little at one end and curved upwards. Use the smile tool for the mouth, pushing it in and down. Roll a ball of red sugarpaste for the nose. For the glasses, make a sausage of black sugarpaste, taper both ends, flatten and place it on the face. Shape a little with a Dresden tool and then paint the glasses with silver edible paste colour.

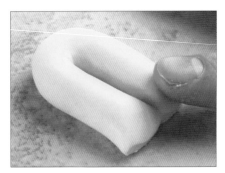

61 Make Santa's legs from yellow sugarpaste, rolled into a sausage. Curl it round, trim and press the ends to create knees. The lower legs will not be seen in the car.

62 Make a long sausage of teddy bear brown sugarpaste for the arms and cut it in half. Taper one end of each and indent by rolling with your little finger to make the wrists and elbows. Press down on the ends to make hands, then cut a thumb with a 'v' shape, and fingers with straight cuts. Dot with a tiny ball tool to make fingernails and cut across diagonally at the shoulder to join on to the body.

63 Make a baseball cap with red sugarpaste. Make a tiny ball, press it down and indent lines with a knife. For the peak, make a ball, flatten it, soften the edge downwards and cut off the back. Stick to the hat. Make a tiny white ball for a pompom.

64 Make a cone in orange sugarpaste for Santa's body and pinch out to hollow the bottom. For the sleeves, make a ball of orange sugarpaste, flatten it and cut it in half. Roll out yellow sugarpaste and use blossom cutters to make the flowers on the shirt. Stick to the body and add centres in red edible pen. For the head, roll a ball and taper it to an egg shape. Add a tiny ball for the nose. Add a moustache and beard as for the Santa on page 17, but shorter. Finally make sunglasses as for Rudolph, but without the silver paint.

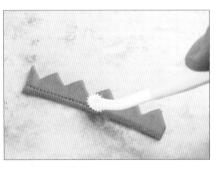

66 Make the penguins as on page 18. Roll orange sugarpaste for the party hats, cut a strip and cut out triangles with a knife. Run a quilting tool along the bottom and wrap the hats round the heads.

65 Make a cone of green sugarpaste for the elf's body. For the arms, make a sausage of white and one of red, cut into sections and reassemble as shown. Make a red ball for the neck. Make two small teardrops of teddy bear brown for hands and cut fingers with a knife. Make a flattened oval for the face, add a tiny ball for a nose. Use a smile tool for the mouth and indent dimples with the handle of a paintbrush. The ears are little cones, stuck on and indented in the same way. Dust the cheeks with rose edible powder food colour (see page 17). Dot the eyes with black edible pen.

This page and opposite

Details from the Christmas Down Under cake.

Index